Bryan Magee, who was born in London in 1930, was educated at Christ's Hospital and (after military service abroad) Keble College, Oxford, where he took two honours degrees – one in Modern History, the other in Philosophy, Politics and Economics – and was President of the Union. After teaching for a year in Sweden, then holding a Fellowship in Philosophy at Yale, he left academic life in 1956 to become a writer, critic and broadcaster. He is a frequent performer on radio and television, and a member of both the music and drama sections of the Critics Circle. He has continued this range of activities since taking up academic work once more in 1970, when he became a Lecturer in Philosophy at Balliol College, Oxford. In 1973 he was elected a Visiting Fellow of All Souls. In 1974 he was elected Member of Parliament for Leyton. His eleven books have been translated into twelve languages, and include *Go West, Young Man* (1958), *The New Radicalism* (1962), *The Democratic Revolution* (1964), *Towards 2000* (1965), *One in Twenty* (1966), *Aspects of Wagner* (1968), *Modern British Philosophy* (1971).

Modern Masters

Popper

Bryan Magee

Fontana/Collins

First published in Fontana 1973
Fourth Impression with corrections April 1975
Eighth Impression August 1979

Copyright © Brian Magee 1973, 1975

Made and printed in Great Britain by
William Collins Sons & Co. Ltd, Glasgow

Short though it is, this book has benefited immeasurably from criticisms of an earlier draft given to me by Lord Boyle, Mr Tyrrell Burgess, Professor Ernest Gellner, Sir Ernst Gombrich, Mr David Miller, Professor John Watkins, Professor Bernard Williams and Sir Karl Popper.

*to Ninian and Libushka
with love*

Contents

Man has created new worlds – of language, of music, of poetry, of science; and the most important of these is the world of the moral demands, for equality, for freedom, and for helping the weak.

The Open Society and Its Enemies,
vol 1, p.65

1 Introductory

Karl Popper is not, as yet anyway, a household name among the educated, and this fact requires explanation. For as Isaiah Berlin writes in his biography of Karl Marx (third edition 1963), Popper's *The Open Society and Its Enemies* contains 'the most scrupulous and formidable criticism of the philosophical and historical doctrines of Marxism by any living writer'; and if this judgment is anywhere near sound, Popper is – in a world one third of whose inhabitants live under governments which call themselves Marxist – a figure of world importance. But quite apart from this he is regarded by many as the greatest living philosopher of science – indeed, Sir Peter Medawar, a winner of the Nobel Prize for Medicine, said on BBC Radio 3 on 28 July 1972: 'I think Popper is incomparably the greatest philosopher of science that has ever been.' Other Nobel Prize winners who have publicly acknowledged his influence on their work include Jacques Monod and Sir John Eccles, who wrote in his book *Facing Reality* (1970): '... my scientific life owes so much to my conversion in 1945, if I may call it so, to Popper's teachings on the conduct of scientific investigations. ... I have endeavoured to follow Popper in the formulation and in the investigation of fundamental problems in neurobiology.' Eccles's advice to other scientists is 'to read and meditate upon Popper's writings on the philosophy of science and to adopt them as the basis of operation of one's scientific life'. Nor is it only experimental scientists who take this view. The distinguished mathematician and theoretical astronomer, Sir Hermann Bondi, has stated simply: 'There is no more to science than its method, and there is no more to its method than Popper has said.' The range of

Popper's intellectual influence, unapproached by that of any English-speaking philosopher now living, extends from members of governments to art historians. In the Preface to *Art and Illusion* (described by Kenneth Clark as 'one of the most brilliant books on art criticism I have ever read') Sir Ernst Gombrich writes: 'I should be proud if Professor Popper's influence were to be felt everywhere in this book.' And progressive Cabinet Ministers in both of the main British political parties, for instance Anthony Crosland and Sir Edward Boyle, have been influenced by Popper in the view they take of political activity.

These examples illustrate, straight away, some important things besides the extraordinary range of application of Popper's work. They show that – unlike that of so many contemporary philosophers – it has a notably *practical* effect on people who are influenced by it: it changes the way they do their own work, and in this and other respects changes their lives. It is, in short, a philosophy of action. Also, it has had such influence on many people who are themselves of first-rate distinction in their own fields. One could scarcely say, then, that Popper is neglected. This underlines all the more, though, the surprisingness of the fact that he is not better known – many lesser thinkers are more famous. This is due partly to chance, partly to unintended misrepresentation of his work, and partly to an aspect of his method which facilitates misapprehension of it by those who have not studied it.

Karl Popper was born in Vienna in 1902. In his early and middle teens he was a Marxist, and then became an enthusiastic Social Democrat. Apart from his studies in science and philosophy he was involved not only in left-wing politics and in social work with children under the aegis of Adler, but also in the Society for Private Concerts founded by Schoenberg. For him, as for so many others, it was a thrilling time and place to be young. After his student days he earned his living as a secondary school teacher in mathematics and physics; but his chief absorptions continued to be social work, left-wing politics, music – and of course philosophy, where he found himself, as he has tended to ever since, at variance with the fashion prevailing in his place and time, which for his generation there and then was the logical positivism of the Vienna Circle. Otto Neurath, a member of the Circle, nicknamed him 'the Official Opposition'. This made him something of an odd man out. He found it impossible to get his early books published in the form in which he wrote them. His first book remains unpublished; and his first and seminal published work, *Logik der Forschung* (published in the autumn of 1934, dated 1935) was a savagely cut version of a book twice as long. It contains the chief of what have since become the generally accepted arguments against logical positivism.

Beneath the surface violence of the political scene in Vienna in the 1930s the left's opposition to fascism was crumbling. Later, in *The Open Society and Its Enemies* (vol ii, pp. 164–165), Popper characterized the radical Marxist view as having been: 'Since the revolution was bound to come, fascism could only be one of the means of bringing it about; and this was more particularly so since the revolution was clearly long overdue. Russia had already had it in spite of its backward economic conditions. Only the vain hopes created by democracy were holding it back in the more advanced countries. Thus the destruction of democracy through the fascists could only promote the revolution by achieving the ultimate disillusionment of the workers in regard to democratic methods. With this, the radical wing of Marxism felt that it had discovered the "essence" and the "true historical role" of fascism. Fascism was, essentially, *the last stand of the bourgeoisie*. Accordingly, the Communists did not fight when the fascists seized power. (Nobody expected the Social Democrats to fight.) For the Communists were sure that the proletarian revolution was overdue and that the fascist interlude, necessary for its speeding up, could not last longer than a few months. Thus no action was required from the Communists. They were harmless. There was never a "communist danger" to the fascist conquest of power.'

Included in the historical reality behind this passage were agonized debates about political strategy and morality in which Popper was involved, and which were the seedbed of much of his later political writing. He came to foresee, with depressing accuracy, the annexation of Austria by Nazi Germany, to be followed by a European war in which his native land would be on the wrong side; and he determined to leave before this happened. (This decision saved his life : for although his childhood had been a Protestant one, and both his parents had been baptized, Hitler would have categorized him as a Jew.) From 1937 to 1945 he taught philosophy at the University of New Zealand. In the earlier part of this period he virtually taught himself Greek in order to study the Greek philosophers, especially Plato. In the middle part he wrote, in English, *The Open Society and Its Enemies* – 'a work,' as Isaiah Berlin says in the source quoted earlier, 'of exceptional originality and power'. Popper regarded this as his war work. The final decision to write it was made on the day he received the news he had so long dreaded, of Hitler's invasion of Austria. This and the fact that the outcome of the Second World War was still uncertain in 1943, when the book was finished, added to the depth of passion which informs this defence of liberty and attack on totalitarianism, whose development and appeal it also attempts to explain. It was published in two volumes in 1945, and brought Popper his first real fame in the English-speaking world.

In 1946 he came to England, where he has lived ever since. In philosophy the prevailing orthodoxy he found on his arrival, in so far as there was one at all, was the logical positivism he had left behind him in Vienna before the war. This had been imported into England in A. J. Ayer's *Lan-*

guage, Truth and Logic, which had been published in January 1936. Popper's own *Logik der Forschung* was still untranslated and virtually unknown; indeed, in so far as it was known *about*, its contents were usually misapprehended. It did not appear in English until the autumn of 1959, a quarter of a century after its original publication, under the title *The Logic of Scientific Discovery*. This translation contained a special preface in which Popper dissociated himself from the (by this time) newly fashionable linguistic philosophy, but *Mind*, the chief journal of linguistic philosophy, reviewed the book uncomprehendingly and without referring to the preface. In his middle age Popper found himself odd man out again in England, just as he had been in Austria in his youth. Nevertheless the solitary international reputation he had long since begun to acquire continued to expand, and he received social recognition in England (he was knighted in 1965). But neither Oxford nor Cambridge wanted him as a Professor. However, he spent the last 23 years of his university career at the London School of Economics, where he became Professor of Logic and Scientific Method.

It was during these years that he released his next two books, both of them collections of articles most of which had already been published. When *The Poverty of Historicism* came out in 1957 Arthur Koestler wrote in *The Sunday Times* that it was 'probably the only book published this year which will outlive this century'. (The set of articles of which it consists had been rejected by *Mind*.) It can be regarded as a pendant to *The Open Society and Its Enemies*. Similarly *Conjectures and Refutations: The Growth of Scientific Knowledge*, published in 1963, can be seen as a pendant to *The Logic of Scientific Discovery*. He has published one more book since his retirement in 1969, another collection of essays called *Objective Knowledge: An Evolutionary Approach*, which came out in 1972. There will probably be several more, for some unpublished books are complete in manuscript; and in addition to the articles, over 100 of them, which have appeared in academic journals, he has an even greater number of articles and written lectures which he has not published. Throughout his life he has been excessively reluctant to let his work go to the printer : there has always been room – and time – for a few more improvements, a few more corrections.

At the beginning of his career the logical positivists saw him as being concerned with essentially the same problems as themselves, and interpreted his work in the light of this assumption. Linguistic philosophers have since done much the same. Both have therefore sincerely believed, and asserted, that his work is nothing like as different from theirs as he himself insists, and they find his insistence tiresome. I shall come to the substance of these misunderstandings in due course. The point I want to make here is that Popper's work itself contains a feature, unavoidable when rightly understood, which has got between him and potential readers – who, being only potential, are not yet in a position to understand it. He believes, in a sense which will be made fully clear later, that only through criticism can knowledge advance. This leads him to put forward most of his important ideas in the course of criticizing other peoples' : for instance, most of his arguments in *The Open Society and Its Enemies* are advanced in criticism of Plato and Marx. One consequence of this is that generations of students have plundered the work for these critiques without reading the book as a whole. It has even come to be widely thought of as *being* a critique of Plato and Marx – with the result that many people who have heard of it but not read it have a mistaken conception of it. Some even assume it, because of its attack on Marx, to be a work of right wing tendencies. The academic controversy it has stirred up has centred not on Popper's positive arguments but on whether his view of other philosophers is valid. Whole books have been written on this, like *In Defense of*

Plato by Ronald B. Levinson, and *The Open Philosophy and The Open Society* by Maurice Cornforth. Argument has ramified through the pages of academic journals about whether Popper's translation of this or that Greek passage faithfully preserves Plato's meaning. The defence of democracy which the book also contains has not received a fraction of this academic attention. Yet even if it could be shown that the treatment of both Plato and Marx is misconceived, the argument in favour of democracy would still be the most powerful in the language. Any intellectually serious criticism of *The Open Society and Its Enemies* should be chiefly concerned with appraising its arguments, not its scholarship – though as I shall illustrate later the scholarship is in any case respectable.

Related to this is another, much slighter obstacle between Popper and possible readers. He believes that philosophy is a necessary activity because we, all of us, take a great number of things for granted, and many of these assumptions are of a philosophical character; we act on them in private life, in politics, in our work, and in every other sphere of our lives – but while some of these assumptions are no doubt true, it is likely that more are false and some are harmful. So the critical examination of our presuppositions – which is a philosophical activity – is morally as well as intellectually important. This view is of philosophy as something lived and important for all of us, not an academic activity or a specialism, and certainly not as consisting primarily in the study of the writings of professional philosophers. Nevertheless it does mean that most of Popper's work consists of the critical examination of theories, and in consequence there is a great deal of discussion of 'isms', and a great many allusions to thinkers of the past, especially in the first works he wrote in English when he was still under the influence of the German academic tradition.

On the other hand few philosophers have taken so much

trouble to be clear. The writing is so clear as to disguise its own depth, and a few readers have mistakenly supposed that what was being said was rather simple, perhaps even a bit obvious. They have missed the thrill of illumination and the excitement to be got from it. The prose itself is massively distinguished: it is magnanimous and humane, with a combination of intellectual and emotional pressure reminiscent of Marx's – there is the same driving force behind the argument, the same sweep and bite, the same bigness and self-confidence, yet a tighter logical rigour. Once the reader has accustomed himself to the terminology it is exhilarating, and has great holding power. Above all – and this is a striking feature of all Popper's work – it is superabundantly rich in arguments.

Popper's is a systematic philosophy in the great central tradition of the subject. But only the most painstaking and unparochial of students could be expected to have read all the various lectures and publications in which it has been presented, in different languages, journals, countries and decades, let alone to see that these are interconnecting parts of a single explanatory framework which extends to the whole of human experience. To take a single example: Popper is an indeterminist in both physics and politics. His argument that it is logically impossible to give a scientific prediction of the future course of history was first put forward in *The British Journal for the Philosophy of Science* in a paper called *Indeterminism in Quantum Physics and in Classical Physics*. Its development in one direction became part of his defence of political freedom and his critique of Marxism; in another it led him to work on a propensity theory of probability which, applied to quantum physics, offers a solution to certain problems in the theory of matter which connect with the historic schism between Einstein, de Broglie and Schrödinger on the one hand and Heisenberg, Niels Bohr and Max Born on the other. Only very few full-time students with the necessary technical equipment are likely to have followed these connections through, and related them to each other.

What I have tried to do in this book is give a bold, clear outline of Popper's thought which exhibits its systematic unity. This involves, for reasons which will become obvious, starting with the theory of knowledge and the philosophy of science. I beg readers who perhaps regard themselves as uninterested in these fields but have opened this book out of an interest in the social and political theories not to skip, for Popper has extended ideas originally worked out in the natural sciences to the social sciences, and a knowledge of the former is indispensable to a deeper understanding of the latter. What is more, I shall be trying to show how the two are parts of a single philosophy which embraces both the natural and the human worlds. I hope also to make it clear why this philosophy has the special influence it does, and in broad terms why it is at odds with other contemporary philosophies – though in a book as short as this it is not possible to go into specific controversies. Nor is it feasible to go into the more technical aspects of physics, probability theory or logic, so I shall not attempt to examine the detailed support from these fields which Popper brings to his general arguments. My concern will be solely with the latter.

2 Scientific Method – the Traditional View and Popper's View

The word 'law' is ambiguous, and anyone who talks of a natural or scientific law being 'broken' is confusing the two main uses of the word. A law of society prescribes what we may or may not do. It can be broken – indeed, if we could not break it there would be no need to have it: society does not legislate against a citizen's being in two places at once. A law of nature, on the other hand, is not prescriptive but descriptive. It tells us what happens – for instance that water boils at 100° Centigrade. As such it purports to be nothing more than a statement of what – given certain initial conditions, such as that there is a body of water and that it is heated – occurs. It may be true or false, but it cannot be 'broken', for it is not a command: water is not being *ordered* to boil at 100° Centigrade. The pre-scientific belief that it was (by some god) is the reason for the unfortunate ambiguity: the laws of nature were thought to be commands of the gods. But nowadays no one would dispute that they are not prescriptions of any kind, to be 'kept' or 'obeyed' or 'broken', but explanatory statements of a general character which purport to be factual and must therefore be modified or abandoned if found to be inaccurate.

The search for natural laws has long been seen as the central task of science, at least since Newton. But the way scientists were supposed to proceed was first systematically described by Francis Bacon. Although his formulation has been much qualified, added to, refined and sophisticated since his day, something in the tradition he pioneered has been accepted by nearly all scientifically minded people from the seventeenth century to the twentieth. It goes like this. The scientist begins by carrying out experiments whose aim is to make carefully controlled and meticulously measured observations at some point on the frontier between our knowledge and our ignorance. He systematically records his findings, perhaps publishes them, and in the course of time he and other workers in the field accumulate a lot of shared and reliable data. As this grows, general features begin to emerge, and individuals start to formulate general hypotheses – statements of a lawlike character which fit all the known facts and explain how they are causally related to each other. The individual scientist tries to confirm his hypothesis by finding evidence which will support it. If he succeeds in verifying it he has discovered another scientific law which will unlock more of the secrets of nature. The new seam is then worked – that is to say the new discovery is applied wherever it is thought it might yield fresh information. Thus the existing stock of scientific knowledge is added to, and the frontier of our ignorance pushed back. And the process begins again on the new frontier.

The method of basing general statements on accumulated observations of specific instances is known as *induction*, and is seen as the hallmark of science. In other words the use of the inductive method is seen as the criterion of demarcation between science and non-science. Scientific statements, being based on observational and experimental evidence – based, in short, on the facts – are contrasted with statements of all other kinds, whether based on authority, or emotion, or tradition, or speculation, or prejudice, or habit, or any other foundation, as alone providing sure and certain knowledge. Science is the corpus of such knowledge, and the growth of science consists in the endless process of adding new certainties to the body of existing ones.

Some awkward questions about this were raised by Hume.

He pointed out that no number of singular observation statements, however large, could logically entail an unrestrictedly general statement. If I observe that event A is attended by event B on one occasion, it does not logically follow that it will be attended by it on any other occasion. Nor would it follow from two such observations – nor from twenty, nor from two thousand. If it happens often enough, said Hume, I may come to expect that the next A will be attended by a B, but this is a fact of psychology, not of logic. The sun may have risen again after every past day of which we have knowledge, but this does not entail that it will rise tomorrow. If someone says : 'Ah yes, but we can in fact predict the precise time at which the sun will rise tomorrow from the established laws of physics, as applied to conditions as we have them at this moment', we can answer him twice over. First, the fact that the laws of physics have been found to hold good in the past does not logically entail that they will continue to hold good in the future. Second, the laws of physics are themselves general statements which are not logically entailed by the observed instances, however numerous, which are adduced in their support. So this attempt to justify induction begs the question by taking the validity of induction for granted. The whole of our science assumes the regularity of nature – assumes that the future will be like the past in all those respects in which natural laws are taken to operate – yet there is no way in which this assumption can be secured. It cannot be established by observation, since we cannot observe future events. And it cannot be established by logical argument, since from the fact that all past futures have resembled past pasts it does not follow that all future futures will resemble future pasts. The conclusion Hume himself came to was that although there is no way of demonstrating the validity of inductive procedures we are so constituted psychologically that we cannot help thinking in terms of them. And since they seem to work in practice we go along with them. This does mean, however, that scientific laws have no rationally secure foundation – neither in logic, nor in experience, since every scientific law, being unrestrictedly general, goes beyond both.

The problem of induction, which has been called 'Hume's problem', has baffled philosophers from his time to our own. C. D. Broad described it as the skeleton in the cupboard of philosophy. Bertrand Russell wrote in his *History of Western Philosophy* (pp. 699–700): 'Hume has proved that pure empiricism is not a sufficient basis for science. But if this one principle [induction] is admitted, everything else can proceed in accordance with the theory that all our knowledge is based on experience. It must be granted that this is a serious departure from pure empiricism, and that those who are not empiricists may ask why, if one departure is allowed, others are to be forbidden. These, however, are questions not directly raised by Hume's arguments. What these arguments prove – and I do not think the proof can be controverted – is, that induction is an independent logical principle, incapable of being inferred either from experience or from other logical principles, and that without this principle science is impossible.'

That the whole of science, of all things, should rest on foundations whose validity it is impossible to demonstrate has been found uniquely embarrassing. It has turned many empirical philosophers into sceptics, or irrationalists, or mystics. Some it has led to religion. Virtually all have felt bound to say, in effect: 'We have to admit that, strictly speaking, scientific laws cannot be proved and are therefore not certain. Even so, their degree of probability is raised by each confirming instance; and in addition to the whole of the known past every moment of the world's continuance brings countless billions of confirming instances – and never a single counter-example. So, if not certain, they are probable to the highest degree which it is possible to conceive; and in practice, if not in theory, this is indistinguishable from certainty.' Nearly all scientists, in so far as they reflect on the logical foundations of what they are doing, go along with this attitude. To them the overwhelmingly important thing is that science delivers the goods – it works, it produces a never-ending stream of useful results: and rather than go on banging their heads against the brick wall of an apparently insoluble logical problem they prefer to get on with doing more science and getting more results. The more philosophically reflective among them, however, have been deeply troubled. For them, and for philosophers generally, induction has presented an unsolved problem at the very foundations of human knowledge, and until such time as it might be solved the whole of science, however intrinsically consistent and extrinsically useful, must be conceded to be somehow floating in mid air, unfixed to *terra firma*.

Popper's seminal achievement has been to offer an acceptable solution to the problem of induction. In doing this he has rejected the whole orthodox view of scientific method outlined so far in this chapter and replaced it with another. It is, of course, this that lies behind the quotations from Medawar, Eccles and Bondi on the first page of this book. And as might be expected of so fundamental an achievement it has proved fruitful beyond the confines of the problem that gave rise to it, and has led to the solution of other important problems.

Popper's solution begins by pointing to a logical asymmetry between verification and falsification. To express it in terms of the logic of statements: although no number of observation statements reporting observations of white swans allows us logically to derive the universal statement 'All swans are white', one single observation statement, reporting one single observation of a black swan, allows us logically to derive the statement 'Not all swans are white.' In this important logical sense empirical generalizations, though not verifiable, are falsifiable. This means that scientific laws are testable in spite of being unprovable: they can be tested by systematic attempts to refute them.

From the beginning Popper drew the distinction between the logic of this situation and the implied methodology. The logic is utterly simple: if a single black swan has been observed then it *cannot* be the case that all swans are white. In *logic*, therefore – that is, if we look at the relation between statements – a scientific law is conclusively falsifiable although it is not conclusively verifiable. *Methodologically* however, we are presented with a different case, for in practice it is always possible to doubt a statement: there may have been some error in the reported observation; the bird in question may have been wrongly identified; or we may decide, *because* it is black, not to categorize it as a swan but to call it something else. So it is always possible for us to refuse, without self-contradiction, to accept the validity of an observation statement. We could thus reject all falsifying experiences whatsoever. But since conclusive falsification is not attainable at the methodological level it is a mistake to ask for it. If we did, and meanwhile kept reinterpreting the evidence to maintain its agreement with our statements, our approach would have become absurdly unscientific. Popper therefore proposes, as an article of method, that we do not systematically evade refutation, whether by introducing *ad hoc* hypotheses, or *ad hoc* definitions, or by always refusing to accept the reliability of inconvenient experimental results, or by any other such device; and that we formulate our theories as unambiguously as we can, so as to expose them as clearly as possible to refutation. On the other hand he also says we should not abandon our theories lightly, for this would involve too uncritical an attitude towards tests, and would mean that the theories themselves were not tested as rigorously as they should be. So although Popper is what might be called a naïve falsificationist at the level of logic he is a highly critical falsificationist at the level of methodology. Much misunderstanding of his work has sprung from a failure to appreciate this distinction.

Let us now consider a practical example. Suppose we start by believing, as most of us are taught at school, that it is a scientific law that water boils at 100° Centigrade. No number of confirming instances will prove this, but we can nevertheless test it by searching for circumstances in which it does not hold. This alone challenges us to think of things which, so far as we know, no one else has hit on. If we are at all imaginative we shall soon discover that water does not boil at 100° Centigrade in closed vessels. So what we thought was a scientific law turns out not to be one. Now at this point we could take a wrong turning. We could salvage our original statement by narrowing its empirical content to 'Water boils at 100° Centigrade in open vessels.' And we could then look systematically for a refutation of our second statement. And if we were rather more imaginative than before we should find it at high altitudes: so that to salvage our second statement we would have to narrow *its* empirical content to 'Water boils at 100° Centigrade in open vessels at sea-level atmospheric pressure.' And we could then begin a systematic attempt to refute our third statement. And so on. In this way we might regard ourselves as pinning down ever more and more precisely our knowledge about the boiling point of water. But to proceed in this way, through a series of statements with vanishing empirical content, would be to miss the most important features of the situation. For when we discovered that water did not boil at 100° Centigrade in closed vessels we had our foot on the threshold of the most important kind of discovery of all, namely the discovery of a new problem: 'Why not?' We are challenged now to produce a hypothesis altogether richer than our original, simple statement, a hypothesis which explains both why water boils at 100° Centigrade in open vessels and also why it does not in closed ones; and the richer the hypothesis is the more it will tell us about the relationship between the two situations, and the more precisely it will enable us to calculate different boiling points. In other words we will now have a second formulation which has not less empirical content than our first but very considerably more. And we should proceed to look systematically for a refutation of *that*. And if, say, we were to find that although it gave us results in both open and closed vessels at sea-level atmospheric pressure it broke down at high altitudes we should have to search for a third hypothesis, richer still, which would explain why each of our first two hypotheses worked, up to the point it did, but then broke down at that point; and also enable us to account for the new situation as well. And then we should test *that*. From each of our successive formulations consequences would be derived which went beyond the existing evidence: our theory, whether true or false, would tell us more about the world than we yet knew. And one of the ways in which we tested it would be by devising confrontations between its consequences and new observable experience; and if we discovered that some of the things it told us were not the case this would be a new discovery: it would add to our knowledge and it would start all over again the search for a better theory.

This, in a nutshell, is Popper's view of the way knowledge advances. There are several things to emphasize. If we had set out to 'verify' our original statement that water boils at 100° Centigrade by accumulating confirming instances of it we should have found no difficulty whatever in accumulating any number of confirming instances we liked, billions and billions of them. But this would not have proved the truth of the statement, nor would it (and this realization may come as something of a shock) have increased the probability of its being true. Worst of all, our accumulation of confirming instances would of itself never have given us reason to doubt, let alone replace, our original statement, and we should never have progressed beyond it. Our knowledge would not have grown as it has – unless in our search for confirming instances we accidentally hit upon a counter-instance. Such an accident would have been the best thing that could have happened to us. (It is in this sense that so many famous discoveries in science have been 'accidental'.) For the growth of our knowledge proceeds from problems and our attempts to solve them. These attempts involve the propounding of theories which, if they are to provide possible solutions at all, must go beyond our existing knowledge, and which therefore require a leap of the imagination. The bolder the theory the more it tells us, and also the more daring the act of imagination. (At the same time, though, the greater is the probability that what the theory tells us is wrong; and we should use rigorous tests to discover whether it is.) Most of the great revolutions in science have turned on theories of breathtaking audacity not only in respect of creative imagination but in the depth of insight involved, and the independence of mind, the un-secured adventurousness of thought, required.

We are now in a position to see why it is inherent in Popper's view that what we call our knowledge is of its nature provisional, and permanently so. At no stage are we able to prove that what we now 'know' is true, and it is always possible that it will turn out to be false. Indeed, it is an elementary fact about the intellectual history of man-kind that most of what has been 'known' at one time or another has eventually turned out to be not the case. So it is a profound mistake to try to do what scientists and philo-sophers have almost always tried to do, namely prove the truth of a theory, or justify our belief in a theory, since this is to attempt the logically impossible. What we can do, however, and this is of the highest possible importance, is to justify our preference for one theory over another. In our successive examples about the boiling of water we were never able to show that our current theory was true, but we were at each stage able to show that it was preferable to our preceding theory. This is the characteristic situation in any of the sciences at any given time. The popular notion that the sciences are bodies of established fact is entirely mistaken. Nothing in science is permanently established, nothing unalterable, and indeed science is quite clearly changing all the time, and not through the accretion of new certainties. If we are rational we shall always base our decisions and expectations on 'the best of our knowledge', as the popular phrase so rightly has it, and provisionally assume the 'truth' of that knowledge *for practical purposes*, because it is the least insecure foundation available; but we shall never lose sight of the fact that at any time experience may show it to be wrong and require us to revise it.

On this view the truth of a statement, by which Popper means (following Tarski) its correspondence to the facts, is a regulative idea. An analogy with the notion of 'accuracy' will make clear what this means. All measurement, whether of time or space, can only be within a certain degree of accuracy. If you order a piece of steel six millimetres long you can have it made accurately to within the finest margin of which the very best instruments are capable, which is now fractions of a millionth of a millimetre. But where, within that margin, the *exact* point of six millimetres lies is something which, in the nature of things, we do not know. It may be that your piece of steel actually is exactly six millimetres long, but you can not know it. All you know is that the length is accurate to within such and such a fraction of a millimetre, and that it is nearer the desired length than anything measurably longer or measurably shorter. With the next improvement in machine tools you may be able to get a piece of steel whose accuracy you can be sure of to within an even closer margin. And another with the next improvement after that. But the notion 'exactly six millimetres', or exactly any other measurement, is not something that can ever be met with in experience. It is a metaphysical notion. But from this it does not follow that mankind cannot make invaluable and prodigious use of measurement; nor that accuracy in measurement, because it is absolutely unattainable, does not matter; nor that we cannot make progress through ever greater and greater degrees of accuracy.

Popper's notion of 'the truth' is very like this: our concern in the pursuit of knowledge is to get closer and closer to the truth, and we may even know that we have made an advance, but we can never know if we have reached our goal. 'We cannot identify science with truth, for we think that both Newton's and Einstein's theories belong to science, but they cannot both be true, and they may well both be false.'[1] One of his favourite quotations is from the pre-Socratic philosopher Xenophanes, which he translates as follows:

The gods did not reveal, from the beginning,
All things to us, but in the course of time
Through seeking we may learn and know things better.
But as for certain truth, no man has known it,
Nor shall he know it, neither of the gods
Nor yet of all the things of which I speak.
For even if by chance he were to utter
The final truth, he would himself not know it:
For all is but a woven web of guesses.

Popper's view of science slides on to its history like a glove. But the particular event which brought home to him the permanently conjectural nature of scientific knowledge was Einstein's challenge to Newton. Newtonian physics was the most successful and important scientific theory ever to be advanced and accepted. Everything in the observable world seemed to confirm it: for more than two centuries its laws were corroborated not just by observation but by

[1] Popper on p. 78 of *Modern British Philosophy* (ed. Bryan Magee).

creative use, for they became the foundation of Western science and technology, yielding marvellously accurate predictions of everything from the existence of new planets down to the movements of the tides and the workings of machinery. If anything was knowledge, this was; the most secure and certain knowledge man had ever acquired about his physical environment. If any scientific laws had been verified inductively as Laws of Nature, these had, by countless billions of observations and experiments. To generation after generation of Western man they were taught as definitive, incorrigible fact. Yet after all this, at the beginning of our own century, a theory different from Newton's was put forward by Einstein. Opinions about the truth of Einstein's theory varied, but its claims to serious attention could not be denied, nor its claim to go beyond Newton's theory in the range of its applications. And this itself is the point. All the observational evidence which fitted Newton's theory (and some about which Newton's theory said nothing) also fitted Einstein's. (In fact it can be logically demonstrated – and had been long ago, by Leibniz – that any finite number of observations can be accommodated within an indefinitely large number of different explanations.) The world had simply been wrong in believing that all that untold evidence *proved* Newton's theory. Yet a whole era of civilization had been based on it, with unprecedented material success. If this amount of verification and inductive support did not prove the truth of a theory, what ever could? And Popper realized that nothing could. He saw that no theory could ever be relied on to be the final truth. The most we can ever say is that it is supported by every observation so far, and yields more, and more precise, predictions than any known alternative. It is still replaceable by a better theory.

If Newton's theory is not a body of truth inherent in the world, and derived by man from the observation of reality, where did it come from? The answer is it came from Newton.[2] It was a man-made hypothesis which fitted all the facts known at the time and from which physicists might have gone on deducing consequences to use and rely on until this got them into intolerable difficulties – though in fact the new theory began to emerge before this point was reached; and there had always been some anomalies in the old theory. A theory might, like Euclid's geometry or Aristotle's logic, be accepted as objective knowledge for over 2000 years, and be almost infinitely fruitful and useful during that time, and yet still in the end be found wanting in some unforeseeable respect, and eventually replaced by a better theory. We now have what most physicists think is an alternative preferable to Newton's theory. But this is still not the final truth. Einstein himself regarded his theory as defective, and spent the second half of his life trying to find a better one. We can expect that one day a theory will be advanced which contains and accounts for Einstein's just as Einstein's contains and accounts for Newton's.

The fact that such theories are not bodies of impersonal facts about the world but are products of the human mind makes them personal achievements of an astonishing order. Scientific creation is not free in the same sense as artistic creation for it has to survive a detailed confrontation with experience: nevertheless the attempt to understand the world is an open task, and as creative geniuses Galileo, Newton and Einstein are on a par with Michelangelo, Shakespeare and Beethoven. An awareness of this, and wonder at it, pervades Popper's work. It is therefore all the more important to be clear about the fact that his theory is an account of the logic and history of science and not of the psychology of its practitioners. He is not under the impression – no one could be – that scientists in general have regarded themselves as doing what he describes. The point

[2] Or rather, according to Popper's theories as explained later, in Chapter 4, from interaction between Newton and World 3. The meaning of this can be left till we come to it.

is that, whether they realize it or not, this is the rationale of what they do, and accounts for the way human knowledge develops. What goes on in the mind of a scientist may be of interest to him, and to people who know him, or to the man who writes his biography, or to people interested in certain aspects of psychology, but it has no bearing on how his work is to be judged. If I were a scientist and published a scientific theory the world would ask questions not about subjective me but about the objective theory. What does it tell us? Is it internally consistent? If so, is it genuinely empirical, or is it tautological? How does it compare with other, already well-tested theories? Does it tell us more than they do? How is *it* to be tested? And so on. People (it could be myself as well as others) will apply it to particular conditions and by deductive processes will derive logical consequences in the form of singular statements which can be tested by observation and experiment. The better it comes out of such tests, and such comparisons with other theories, the better corroborated we shall regard it as being.

About this process as a whole there are three points to stress. First, how I arrived at the theory has no bearing on its scientific or logical status. Second, the observations and experiments in question, far from giving rise to the theory, are partially derived from it, and are designed to test it. Third, at no point does induction come into the matter. The traditional view of the way we think, and of scientific method, gave rise to the problem of induction, but the traditional view was radically mistaken and can be replaced, as here, by a more accurate one within which the problem of induction does not arise. So induction, Popper is saying, is a dispensable concept, a myth. It does not exist. There is no such thing.

A critic might object that Popper has excluded from consideration the very process in which induction does occur, namely the process of theory-formation. Granted, our critic might say, that singular observations cannot *entail* a gene-

ral theory, they may nevertheless *suggest* one, especially to
a scientist of insight and imagination; so *in fact* theories can
be, and are, arrived at by generalization from observed
instances. Admittedly, he may say, there is always a
'jump' involved from the singular to the general; but the
process is not a purely random or irrational one : there is a
kind of logic involved, and it is this that we call induction.

Popper's reply is as follows. From the fact that it is of no
scientific or logical significance how a theory is arrived at it
follows that no way is illegitimate, and therefore perfectly
good theories may well be arrived at in the way the critic
describes. However, the description is of a psychological
process, not a logical one. And in fact this whole problem
of induction has its roots in a failure to distinguish logical
from psychological processes. We have accounts from
scientists of their having arrived at theories in any number
of different ways : in dreams or dreamlike states; in flashes
of inspiration; even as a result of misunderstandings and
mistakes. If one pursues the point, a study of the history of
science leaves no doubt that most theories are arrived at not
in any of these ways, and not by generalizing from experimental observations either, but by modifying already-
existing theories. There can no more be a *logic of creation*
in the sciences than there can be such a thing in the arts.
'It so happens that my arguments in this book [*The Logic
of Scientific Discovery*, p. 32] are quite independent of this
problem. However, my view of the matter, for what it is
worth, is that there is no such thing as a logical method
of having new ideas, or a logical reconstruction of this process. My view may be expressed by saying that every
discovery contains "an irrational element", or "a creative
intuition", in Bergson's sense. In a similar way Einstein
speaks of the "search for those highly universal laws ...
from which a picture of the world can be obtained by
pure deduction. There is no logical path", he says, "leading

to these ... laws. They can only be reached by intuition, based upon something like an intellectual love ('*Einfühlung*') of the objects of experience." ' In a letter to Popper which is printed as an appendix to the English translation of *Logik der Forschung* Einstein states quite explicitly his agreement with Popper 'that theory cannot be fabricated out of the results of observation, but that it can only be invented'.

What is more, observation as such cannot be prior to theory as such, since some theory is presupposed by any observation. Failure to recognize this is, in Popper's view, the flaw in the foundations of the empirical tradition. 'The belief that science proceeds from observation to theory is still so widely and so firmly held that my denial of it is often met with incredulity.... But in fact the belief that we can start with pure observations alone, without anything in the nature of a theory, is absurd; as may be illustrated by the story of the man who dedicated his life to natural science, wrote down everything he could observe, and bequeathed his priceless collection of observations to the Royal Society to be used as inductive evidence.... Twenty-five years ago I tried to bring home the same point to a group of physics students in Vienna by beginning a lecture with the following instructions: "Take pencil and paper; carefully observe, and write down what you have observed!" They asked, of course, *what* I wanted them to observe. Clearly the instruction, "Observe!" is absurd.... Observation is always selective. It needs a chosen object, a definite task, an interest, a point of view, a problem. And its description presupposes a descriptive language, with property words; it presupposes similarity and classification, which in its turn presupposes interests, points of view, and problems.'[3] This means 'that observations, and even more so observation statements and statements of experimental results, are always *interpretations* of the facts obser-

[3] *Conjectures and Refutations*, p. 46.

ved; that they are *interpretations in the light of theories*'.[4]

At every level, then, our knowledge can consist only of our theories. And our theories are the products of our minds. Even the concepts with which we think are not, as empiricists from Locke and Hume to the present day have believed, 'given' to us from outside by objective regularities in our environment, but are developed by us in response to our own problems, interests and points of view: like our knowledge they too are made, not found. But of a concept it cannot be asked, as it can of a theory, whether it is true or false; and the asking of 'what is?' questions about concepts ('what is life?' ... 'What is mind?') leads to sterile analysis and verbalism (more of this in the next chapter). So we should eschew the elucidation of concepts for the testing of theories. And when it comes to this 'the problem "Which comes first, the hypothesis (*H*) or the observation (*O*)," is soluble; as is the problem, "Which comes first, the hen (*H*) or the egg (*O*)". The reply to the latter is, "An earlier kind of egg"; to the former, "An earlier kind of hypothesis". It is quite true that any particular hypothesis we choose will have been preceded by observations – the observations, for example, which it is designed to explain. But these observations, in their turn, presupposed the adoption of a frame of reference: a frame of expectations: a frame of theories. If they were significant, if they created a need for explanation and thus gave rise to the invention of a hypothesis, it was because they could not be explained within the old theoretical framework, the old horizon of expectations. There is no danger here of an infinite regress. Going back to more and more primitive theories and myths we shall in the end find unconscious, *inborn* expectations.'[5]

It will be seen that at this point Popper's theory of knowledge merges into a theory of evolution. We shall take up the connection, after the next chapter, in Chapter 4.

[4] *The Logic of Scientific Discovery*, p. 107n.
[5] *Conjectures and Refutations*, p. 47.

3 The Criterion of Demarcation between what is and what is not Science

According to what I have called the traditional view, what distinguishes science from non-science is the use of inductive method. But if there is no such thing as induction this cannot be the criterion of demarcation. What is, then? One way of reaching Popper's answer to this question is by pursuing the contrast with the view he replaced.

According to the traditional, inductivist view, what scientists are looking for are statements about the world which have the maximum degree of probability, given the evidence. Popper denies this. Any fool, he points out, can produce an indefinite number of predictions with a probability almost equal to 1 – propositions like 'It will rain', which are practically bound to be true and can never be proved false – never, because however many millions of years go by without a drop of rain it may still remain true that it will, one day, rain. The probability of such statements is maximal because the informative content is minimal. Indeed, there are true statements whose probability is equal to 1 and whose informative content is nil, namely tautologies, which tell us nothing at all about the world because they are necessarily true regardless of the way things are.

If we make the statement in our above example falsifiable by restricting it to a finite time span – 'It will rain some time in the next year' – it is still virtually bound to be true, even though it can now be proved false; so it remains unhelpful. If we add to its content further, say by making it refer to a particular area – 'It will rain in England some time in the next year' – we are at last beginning to say something, because there are quite a number of places on the earth's surface where it will not rain in the next year. Now, for the first time, some worthwhile information is being conveyed. And the more specific we make our statement – we can narrow it down to 'It will rain in England in the next week', then to 'It will rain in London in the next week', and so on – the more probable that it will prove wrong, but at the same time the more informative and, if true, useful it becomes – until we get to statements like 'It will rain in central London this afternoon', which may be very far from obvious (at noon on a cloudless summer day) and are of real practical usefulness.

What we are interested in, then, are statements with a high informative content, this consisting of all the non-tautological propositions which can be deduced from them. But the higher the informative content the lower the probability, according to the probability calculus; for the more information a statement contains, the greater the number of ways in which it may turn out to be false. Just as any fool can produce statements of a very high probability which tell us practically nothing, so any fool can produce statements with a very high informative content if he is not bothered about whether they are false. What we want are statements of a high informative content, and therefore low probability, which nevertheless come close to the truth. And it is precisely such statements that scientists are interested in. The fact that they are highly falsifiable makes them also highly testable: informative content, which is in inverse proportion to probability, is in direct proportion to testability. The true statement with the highest possible informative content would be a full, specific and accurate description of the world; and every possible observation or experience would constitute a test, a potential falsification, of it; and the probability of its being true would be unimaginably close to zero, since the number of ways in which it was possible that things were otherwise would be also the highest possible. 'It is not truisms which science unveils. Rather, it is part of the greatness and the beauty of science that we can learn, through our own critical investigations, that the world is utterly different from what we ever imagined – until our imagination was fired by the refutation of our earlier theories.'[1]

A sense of awe at science and the world it reveals is to be found even in Popper's writings on politics. In *The Poverty of Historicism* (p. 56) he says : 'Science is most significant as one of the greatest spiritual adventures that man has yet known.' This is like a form of the religious sense, though Popper is perhaps not what people usually mean by a religious man; for it is, after all, central to most religious beliefs that behind the world of appearances, the everyday world of common sense and ordinary human observation and experience, there is a reality of a different order which sustains that world and presents it to our senses. Now it is precisely such a reality that science reveals – a world of unobservable entities and invisible forces, waves, cells, particles, all interlockingly organized and structured down to a deeper level than anything we have yet been able to penetrate. Men presumably always have looked at flowers and been moved by their beauty and their smell : but only since the last century has it been possible to take a flower in your hand and know that you have between your fingers a complex association of organic compounds containing carbon, hydrogen, oxygen, nitrogen, phosphorus, and a great many other elements, in a complex structure of cells, all of which have evolved from a single cell; and to know something of the internal structure of these cells, and the processes by which they evolved, and the genetic processes by which this flower was begun, and will produce other flow-

[1] *The Logic of Scientific Discovery*, p. 431.

ers; to know in detail how the light from it is reflected to your eye; and to know details of those workings of your eye, and your nose, and your neurophysiological system, which enable you to see and smell and touch the flower. These inexhaustible and almost incredible realities which are all around us and within us are recent discoveries which are still being explored, while similar new discoveries continue to be made; and we have before us an endless vista of such new possibilities stretching into the future, all of it beyond man's wildest dreams until almost the age we ourselves are living in. Popper's ever-present and vivid sense of this, and of the fact that every discovery opens up new problems for us, informs his theoretical methodology. He knows that our ignorance grows with our knowledge, and that we shall therefore always have more questions than answers. He knows that interesting truth consists of quite staggeringly unlikely propositions, not to be even conjectured without a rare boldness of imagination. And he knows that such adventurous hypotheses are far more likely to be wrong than right, and can not be even provisionally accepted until we have made a serious attempt to find out what might be wrong with them. He knows that if, on the other hand, we reach for the most probable explanation every time we come up against a problem it will always be that *ad hoc* explanation which goes least beyond existing evidence, and therefore gets us least far. Bolder theorizing, though it will get us further if proved right, is more likely to be proved wrong. But that is not to be feared. 'The wrong view of science betrays itself in the craving to be right.'[2]

The realization that this is so can have a liberating effect on the working scientist which Sir John Eccles has headily described. 'The erroneous belief that science eventually leads to the certainty of a definitive explanation carries with it the implication that it is a grave scientific mis-

[2] *The Logic of Scientific Discovery*, p. 281.

demeanour to have published some hypothesis that eventually is falsified. As a consequence scientists have often been loath to admit the falsification of such an hypothesis, and their lives may be wasted in defending the no longer defensible. Whereas according to Popper, falsification in whole or in part is the anticipated fate of all hypotheses, and we should even rejoice in the falsification of an hypothesis that we have cherished as our brain-child. One is thereby relieved from fears and remorse, and science becomes an exhilarating adventure where imagination and vision lead to conceptual developments transcending in generality and range the experimental evidence. The precise formulation of these imaginative insights into hypotheses opens the way to the most rigorous testing by experiment, it being always anticipated that the hypothesis may be falsified and that it will be replaced in whole or in part by another hypothesis of greater explanatory power.'[3]

Not only working scientists may be liberated in this way. For all of us, in all our activities, the notions that we can do better only by finding out what can be improved and then improving it; and therefore that shortcomings are to be actively sought out, not concealed or passed over; and that critical comment from others, far from being resented, is an invaluable aid to be insisted on and welcomed, are liberating to a remarkable degree. It may be difficult to get people – conditioned to resent criticism and expect it to be resented, and therefore to keep silent about both their own mistakes and others' – to provide the criticisms on which improvement depends; but no one can possibly give us more service than by showing us what is wrong with what we think or do; and the bigger the fault, the bigger the improvement made possible by its revelation. The man who welcomes and acts on criticism will prize it almost above friendship : the man who fights it out of concern to maintain his position is clinging to non-growth. Anything like a

[3] J. C. Eccles: *Facing Reality*, p. 107.

widespread changeover in our society towards Popperian attitudes to criticism would constitute a revolution in social and interpersonal relationships – not to mention organizational practice, which we shall come to later.

But to return to the scientist: his critical search for better and better theories imposes high demands on any he is prepared to entertain. A theory must first of all provide a solution to a problem that interests us. But it must also be compatible with all known observations, and contain its predecessor theories as first approximations – though it must also contradict them at the points where they failed, and account for their failure. (Herein, incidentally, lies the explanation of the continuity of science.) If in a given problem situation more than one theory is put forward which does all these things we have to try to decide between them. The fact that they are different may mean that from one of them it is possible to deduce testable propositions which are not deducible from the other; and this may make our preference empirically decidable. If other things remain equal our preference will always be, after tests, for the theory with the higher informative content, both because it has been better tested and because it tells us more: such a theory is better corroborated as well as more useful. 'By the degree of corroboration of a theory I mean a concise report evaluating the state (at a certain time *t*) of the critical discussion of a theory, with respect to the way it solves its problems; its degree of testability; the severity of tests it has undergone; and the way it has stood up to these tests. Corroboration (or degree of corroboration) is thus an evaluating *report of past performance*. Like preference, it is essentially comparative: in general, one can only say that the theory A has a higher (or lower) degree of corroboration than a competing theory B, in the light of the critical discussion, which includes testing, *up to some time t.*'[4] So at any given time, among competing theories, it is the

[4] *Objective Knowledge*, p. 18.

best corroborated theory with the highest informative content that gives the best results and is therefore, or should be, the prevailing one.

The point has been made that at any given time the overwhelming majority of scientists are not trying to overthrow the prevailing orthodoxy at all but are working happily within it. They are not innovating, and they seldom have to choose between competing theories: what they are doing is putting accepted theories to work. This is what has come to be known as 'normal science', from Thomas S. Kuhn's use of the phrase in *The Structure of Scientific Revolutions* (second edition 1970). The point is a valid one, I think, but it is not a point against Popper. It is true that Popper's writings are somewhat loftily exclusive in their references to the pathbreaking geniuses of science, whose activities his theories most obviously fit. And it is also true that most scientists take for granted, in order to solve problems at a lower level, theories which only a few of their colleagues are questioning. But at that lower level their activities will be found to be open to the Popperian analysis, which is essentially a logic of problem solving. Popper has always been primarily concerned with discovery and innovation, and therefore with the testing of theories and the growth of knowledge: Kuhn is concerned with how the people who apply these theories and this knowledge go about their work. Popper has always been careful to make the distinction, drawn already in this book, between the logic of scientific activities and their psychology, sociology, and so forth: Kuhn's theory is in fact a sociological theory about the working activity of scientists in our society. It is not irreconcilable with Popperism, and what is more, Kuhn has modified it considerably in Popper's direction since he first put it forward. Readers who want to pursue this question are referred to the symposium *Criticism and the Growth of Knowledge*.[5]

[5] Ed. Lakatos and Musgrave, Cambridge University Press, 1970.

Talking as we now are of the uses to which theories are put brings us to the matter of their truth content, this being Popper's term for the class of true statements which follow from a theory. It is important to realize that all empirical statements, including false ones, have a truth content. For instance, let us suppose that today is Monday. Then the statement 'Today is Tuesday' is false. Yet from this false statement it follows that 'Today is not Wednesday', 'Today is not Thursday', and many other statements which are true. True, in fact, are an *indefinite* number of other statements which follow from our false one: for instance 'The French name for this day of the week contains five letters', or 'Today is not early closing day in Oxford'. Every false statement has an indefinite number of true consequences – which is why, in argument, disproving an opponent's premises does nothing to refute his conclusions. More to the point, it is why a scientific theory which is not true may lead us to a great many conclusions which are – more, it may be, than any of its predecessors – and therefore be highly important and useful. Of course, most of the truth content of any theory will be either trivial or irrelevant to our particular purposes: what we want, obviously, is relevant or useful truth content. But we may even get more of this from a false statement than from a true one. Suppose it is now one minute to noon: then the statement: 'It is twelve o'clock precisely' is false. Yet for almost every purpose I can think of this false statement has more relevant and useful truth content than the true statement 'The time is now between ten in the morning and four in the afternoon'. Likewise in science: for most purposes a clearcut statement which is slightly out is more serviceable than one which is true but vague, I am not, obviously, suggesting that we should rest content with false statements. But scientists are commonly in the position of having to use a theory which they know to be faulty, because there is as yet no better one available.

As I said earlier, Popper recommends that we formulate our theories in as clearcut a way as possible, so as to expose them most unambiguously to refutation. And at the methodological level we should not, he says, (see page 23) systematically evade refutation by continually reformulating either our theory or our evidence in order to keep the two in accord. This is what many Marxists do, and many psychoanalysts. Thus they are substituting dogmatism for science while claiming to be scientific. A scientific theory is not one which explains everything that can possibly happen : on the contrary, it rules out most of what could possibly happen, and is therefore itself ruled out if what it rules out happens. So a genuinely scientific theory places itself permanently at risk. And here we come to Popper's answer to the question raised at the beginning of this chapter. *Falsifiability is the criterion of demarcation between science and non-science.* The central point is that if all possible states of affairs fit in with a theory then no actual state of affairs, no observations, no experimental results, can be claimed as supporting evidence for it. There is no observable difference between its being true and its being false. So it conveys no scientific information. Only if some imaginable observation would refute it is it testable. And only if it is testable is it scientific.

I have mentioned Marxism and psychoanalysis at this point because it was consideration of these, among other theories, that led the young Popper to his criterion of demarcation. He was thrilled and impressed by the way Einstein's theory of relativity seemed to expose itself nakedly to refutation by predicting observable effects which no one would have dreamt of expecting. The General Theory (and incidentally Einstein's progress from the Special to the General Theory is the subject of an uncompleted book of Popper's) led to the conclusion that light must be attracted by heavy bodies. Einstein saw that if this were correct then light which travels close to the sun on its way from a star to the earth must be deflected by the gravitational pull of the sun. Normally in daytime we cannot see such stars, because of the sun's brilliance, but if we could, the deflection of their light-rays would make them appear to be in different positions from those we know them to occupy. And the predicted difference could be checked by photographing a fixed star in such circumstances by day, and then again at night when the sun was not there. Eddington tested this by one of the most famous scientific observations of the century. In 1919 he led an expedition to a point in Africa from which, he calculated, a forthcoming eclipse of the sun was about to render such stars visible, and hence photographable, by day. On 29th May the observations were made. And they corroborated Einstein's theory. Other theories which claimed to be scientific and were at the height of intellectual fashion in the Vienna of Popper's youth, such as those of Freud and Adler, did not, and could not be made to, put their lives at stake in this way. No conceivable observations could contradict them. They would explain whatever occurred (though differently). And Popper saw that their ability to explain everything, which so convinced and excited their adherents, was precisely what was most wrong with them.

The only other fashionable theory of scientific pretensions and comparable appeal, Marxism, was in a different case. Falsifiable predictions were indeed deducible from it. The trouble was that a number of such predictions had already been falsified. But Marxists refused to accept the falsification, and never-endingly reformulated the theory (and the evidence) to keep falsification at bay. With them, in practice, as with the psychoanalysts in theory, their ideas had the unfalsifiable certainty of a religious faith, and the insistence that they were scientific was, however sincere, mistaken.

Popper often pointed out that the secret of the enormous psychological appeal of these various theories lay in their ability to explain everything. To know in advance that whatever happens you will be able to understand it gives you not only a sense of intellectual mastery but, even more important, an emotional sense of secure orientation in the world. Acceptance of one of these theories had, he observed, 'the effect of an intellectual conversion or revelation, opening your eyes to a new truth hidden from those not yet initiated. Once your eyes were thus opened you saw confirming instances everywhere: the world was full of *verifications* of the theory. Whatever happened always confirmed it. Thus its truth appeared manifest; and unbelievers were clearly people who did not want to see the manifest truth; who refused to see it, either because it was against their class interest, or because of their repressions which were still "un-analysed" and crying aloud for treatment. ... A Marxist could not open a newspaper without finding on every page confirming evidence for his interpretation of history; not only in the news, but also in its presentation – which revealed the class bias of the paper – and especially of course in what the paper did *not* say. The Freudian analysts emphasized that their theories were constantly verified by their "clinical observations". As for Adler, I was much impressed by a personal experience. Once, in 1919, I reported to him a case which to me did not seem particularly Adlerian, but which he found no difficulty in analysing in terms of his theory of inferiority feelings, although he had not even seen the child. Slightly shocked, I asked him how he could be so sure. "Because of my thousandfold experience," he replied; whereupon I could not help saying: "And with this new case, I suppose, your experience has become thousand-and-one-fold." '[6]

Popper has never – and this cannot be too strongly emphasized – dismissed such theories as valueless, still less as nonsense. From the beginning, large numbers of people, associating him with the logical positivists, supposed that

[6] *Conjectures and Refutations*, pp. 34-35.

he did, and in consequence misunderstood what he was saying. 'This does not mean that Freud and Adler were not seeing certain things correctly : I personally do not doubt that much of what they say is of considerable importance, and may well play its part one day in a psychological science which is testable. But it does mean that those "clinical observations" which analysts naïvely believe confirm their theory cannot do this any more than the daily confirmations which astrologers find in their practice. And as for Freud's epic of the Ego, the Super-ego, and the Id, no substantially stronger claim to scientific status can be made for it than for Homer's collected stories from Olympus. These theories describe some facts, but in the manner of myths. They contain most interesting psychological suggestions, but not in a testable form.

'At the same time I realized that such myths may be developed, and become testable; that historically speaking all – or very nearly all – scientific theories originate from myths, and that a myth may contain important anticipations of scientific theories. Examples are Empedocles' theory of evolution by trial and error, or Parmenides' myth of the unchanging block universe in which nothing ever happens and which, if we add another dimension, becomes Einstein's block universe (in which, too, nothing ever happens, since everything is, four-dimensionally speaking, determined and laid down from the beginning). I thus felt that if a theory is found to be non-scientific, or "metaphysical" (as we might say), it is not thereby found to be unimportant, or insignificant, or "meaningless", or "nonsensical". But it cannot claim to be backed by empirical evidence in the scientific sense – although it may easily be, in some genetic sense, the "result of observation".'[7]

The first widespread misunderstanding of Popper's work, extensively and still propagated in print, consisted in seeing him as advancing falsifiability as the criterion of demarca-

[7] *Conjectures and Refutations*, pp. 37–38.

tion not, as in fact he was, between science and non-science, but between sense and nonsense – and then (because the misunderstanders themselves believed that what was not science was nonsense) to insist in answer to protest that it came to much the same thing in the end anyway. For the logical positivists, determined to clear away the metaphysical verbiage with which philosophy had become clogged, were centrally concerned to find a principle of demarcation between statements which really did say something and statements which did not. And they arrived at the view that significant propositions were of two kinds. There were statements in logic and mathematics, which did not purport to give information about the empirical world and could therefore be established as true or false without reference to experience: the true ones were tautologies and the false ones selfcontradictions. And there were statements which did purport to give information about the empirical world whose truth or falsehood must therefore make some observable difference to something, and so could be established by observation. Every statement which was not a formal proposition in mathematics or logic (which Bertrand Russell had tried to show were the same thing) and was also not empirically verifiable must be meaningless. Verifiability, thus, was held to be the criterion of demarcation between meaningful and meaningless statements about the world.

Popper from the beginning attacked this on several grounds. First, whether or not singular statements were empirically verifiable, universal statements such as scientific laws were certainly not, so the verification principle eliminated not only metaphysics but the whole of natural science. Second, the verification principle pronounced all metaphysics to be meaningless, yet historically it is out of metaphysics – out of superstitious, mythical and religious conceptions of the world – that science has emerged. An idea which is at one time untestable, and therefore metaphysical, may with changed circumstances become testable and therefore scientific. 'Examples of such ideas are atomism; the idea of a single physical "principle" or ultimate element (from which the others derive); the theory of terrestrial motion (opposed by Bacon as fictitious); the age-old corpuscular theory of light; the fluid-theory of electricity (revived as the electron-gas hypothesis of metallic conduction).'[8] Not only can a metaphysical theory be meaningful, it may actually be true; but if we have no way of testing it there can be no empirical evidence for it, and therefore it cannot be held to be scientific. Even so, theories which cannot be empirically tested may still be critically discussed, and have the arguments for and against them compared, as a result of which one of them may appear preferable to another. So far from regarding metaphysics as nonsense, Popper always declared himself to hold metaphysical beliefs, for instance about the existence of regularities in nature. A third and devastating point he made against the logical positivists was that if verifiable and tautologous assertions alone are held to be meaningful then any debate about the concept of 'meaning' must contain meaningless statements.

It was the prolonged inability of logical positivists to meet arguments such as these that led eventually to the withering away of logical positivism. But at first, and for a long time, they mistook Popper by understanding him in their own terms. Because he was arguing with them about topics of central importance to them they took him to be a philosopher of the same kind as themselves; and because their chief aim was to find a criterion of demarcation between sense and nonsense, and they were becoming uncomfortably aware of the force of some of the arguments against verifiability, they took him to be ingeniously proposing falsifiability instead; and many of their arguments against him rest on this false assumption. As I have already

[8] *The Logic of Scientific Discovery*, p. 278.

remarked, because of this obsession with meaning, and their inflexible view that unscientific theories were meaningless, they met his assertion that he was in fact proposing something entirely different with the protest that it really came to much the same in the end. The truth is that Popper was never a positivist of any kind; quite the reverse, he was the decisive anti-positivist, the man who put forward from the beginning the arguments that led (after an excessively long time) to logical positivism's dissolution. The totally different nature of his approach from theirs may be illustrated by the simplest of examples: the logical positivists would have said that 'God exists' is just meaningless noise, exhaust; Popper would have said that it is a statement which has meaning and could be true, but because there is no conceivable way in which it might be falsified it is not a scientific statement.

Not only was Popper not putting forward a criterion of meaning: he has always held that to do so is a major philosophical error. He also believes that habitual discussion of the meanings of words is not only boring but harmful. The notion that we must define our terms before we can have a useful discussion is, he holds, demonstrably incoherent, for every time one defines a term one has to introduce new terms in the definition (otherwise the definition is circular) and one is then required to define the new terms. So we can never get to the discussion at all, because we can never complete the necessary preliminaries. Discussion, then, has to make use of undefined terms. Similarly the notion that precise knowledge requires precise definition is demonstrably wrong. Physicists are not in the habit of debating the meaning of terms like 'energy', 'light', and all the other concepts they habitually employ. Precise analysis and definition of such terms would present inexhaustible difficulties, and physicists leave them for the most part undefined. Yet the most accurate and extensive knowledge we have is in the physical sciences. Another point to be made about good definitions in science is that they are, as Popper puts it, properly to be read from right to left and not from left to right. The sentence 'A di-neutron is an unstable system comprising two neutrons' is the scientists' answer to the question 'What shall we call an unstable system comprising two neutrons?', not an answer to the question 'What is a di-neutron?' The word 'di-neutron' is a handy substitute for a long description, that is all: no information about physics is to be gained from analysing it. Physics would go on exactly the same without it: only communication would have been made a little more cumbersome. 'The view that the precision of science and of scientific language depends upon the precision of its terms is certainly very plausible, but it is none the less, I believe, a mere prejudice. The precision of a language depends, rather, just upon the fact that it takes care not to burden its terms with the task of being precise. A term like "sand-dune" or "wind" is certainly very vague. (How many inches high must a little sand-hill be in order to be called "sand-dune"? How quickly must the air move in order to be called "wind"?) However, for many of the geologist's purposes, these terms are quite sufficiently precise; and for other purposes, when a higher degree of differentiation is needed, he can always say "dunes between 4 and 30 feet high" or "wind of a velocity of between 20 and 40 miles an hour". And the position in the more exact sciences is analogous. In physical measurements, for instance, we always take care to consider the range within which there may be an error; and precision does not consist in trying to reduce this range to nothing, or in pretending that there is no such range, but rather in its explicit recognition.'[9]

If one wanted to be provocative one might assert that the amount of worthwhile knowledge that comes out of any field of enquiry (except of course language studies) tends to be in inverse proportion to the amount of discussion about

[9] *The Open Society and Its Enemies*, vol. ii, pp. 19–20.

the meanings of words that goes on in it. Such discussion, far from being necessary to clear thinking and precise knowledge, obscures both, and is bound to lead to endless argument about words instead of about matters of substance. Language is an instrument, and what matters is what is done with it – in this case its use to formulate and discuss theories about the world. A philosopher who devotes his life to a concern with the instrument is like a carpenter who devotes all his working time to sharpening up his tools but never uses them except on each other. Philosophers, like everyone else, have a duty to speak clearly and directly; but like the physicists they should do their work in such a way that nothing of importance depends on the way they use words.

From this standpoint Popper consistently attacked both of the philosophies fathered by Wittgenstein – the logical positivism that developed out of logical atomism and dominated one generation; and the linguistic analysis that dominated the next. 'Language analysts believe that there are no genuine philosophical problems, or that the problems of philosophy, if any, are problems of linguistic usage, or of the meaning of words. I, however, believe that there is at least one philosophical problem in which all thinking men are interested. It is the problem of cosmology : *the problem of understanding the world – including ourselves, and our knowledge, as part of the world.* All science is cosmology, I believe, and for me the interest of philosophy, no less than of science, lies solely in the contributions which it has made to it.'[10]

Many different twofold distinctions have been applied in the history of philosophy (e.g. nominalist/realist; empiricist/transcendentalist; materialist/idealist) and none of them should be driven too hard : what can make them particularly misleading is that, whichever of them is applied,

[10] Preface to the 1959 edition of *The Logic of Scientific Discovery*.

large-scale figures usually straddle the divide. But one of the dualisms which runs through most of the subject's history is that between a view of philosophy which sees it as an attempt to understand our use of concepts, and a view of philosophy which sees it as an attempt to understand the world. Obviously it is impossible to understand the world without the use of concepts, and therefore people on both sides of the distinction will usually believe with some justification that they are doing both jobs. Nevertheless the difference of emphasis is often extreme. It was the famous distinction in the Middle Ages between the (to us, now, misleadingly named) realists, who were of the first kind ('concepts are real entities in themselves, and come before particulars: the latter derive from and depend on the former') and the nominalists, who were of the second kind ('concepts function as names for things, which are therefore prior: the labels can be changed without changing reality'). For most of this century philosophy in the English-speaking world has been weighted heavily towards the elucidation of concepts. Popper is very much a philosopher of the other kind (although he is a realist in today's sense of the word, the sense of believing that a material world exists independently of experience).

At the very beginning of *My Philosophical Development* Bertrand Russell tells how, until about 1917 – by which time he was 45 and had done nearly all the philosophical work for which he is now famous – he 'had thought of language as transparent – that is to say, as a medium which could be employed without paying attention to it'. Wittgenstein, on the other hand, was obsessed with language, and in particular with meaning, all his life. His first book, *Tractatus Logico-Philosophicus*, which was published in 1921, was the text most influential on the Vienna Circle. He came subsequently to regard it as mistaken, and mistaken precisely because it incorporated a false theory of meaning. He thereupon set out to investigate the different sorts of ways in which we can be misled by our own use of language, having been so misled himself, and this nourished a new school of philosophy, usually called 'linguistic analysis'. Wittgenstein's chief book in this vein, *Philosophical Investigations*, published posthumously in 1953, has probably had more influence on British philosophy since the Second World War than any other book. (The runner up, Gilbert Ryle's *The Concept of Mind*, was itself profoundly influenced by the later Wittgenstein.)

On page 216 of *My Philosophical Development* Russell wrote: 'During the period since 1914 three philosophies have successively dominated the British philosophical world: first that of Wittgenstein's *Tractatus*, second that of the Logical Positivists, and third that of Wittgenstein's *Philosophical Investigations*. Of these, the first had very considerable influence upon my own thinking, though I do not now think that this influence was wholly good. The second school, that of the Logical Positivists, had my general sympathy though I disagreed with some of its most distinctive doctrines. The third school, which for convenience I shall designate as WII to distinguish it from the doctrines of the *Tractatus* which I shall call WI, remains to me completely unintelligible. Its positive doctrines seem to me trivial and its negative doctrines unfounded. I have not found in Wittgenstein's *Philosophical Investigations* anything that seemed to me interesting and I do not understand why a whole school finds important wisdom in its pages.' Russell became increasingly alienated from his professional colleagues as he grew older. On page 214 of *My Philosophical Development* he wrote of 'Wittgenstein, by whom I was superseded in the opinion of many British philosophers. . . . It is not an altogether pleasant experience to find oneself regarded as antiquated after having been, for a time, in the fashion. It is difficult to accept this experience gracefully.' But at least he had done his great work, and acquired his great reputation, before Wittgenstein became

known. Popper, who explicitly shares Russell's view of the
later Wittgenstein,[11] had no chance of doing so. And it has
been his quite peculiar misfortune, in Austria as well as
England, to live the bulk of his professional life in Wittgen-
stein-dominated places and times. This is the key to the
otherwise baffling underestimation of him by his professional colleagues when this is contrasted with his influence
outside his own profession, and on so many such gifted
people. As Geoffrey Warnock has said[12]: 'Philosophers tend
very much to take up the subject in the state in which they
find it, and to swim contentedly along in the way the
stream is going.' But in one respect Popper's experience
looks like being the opposite of Russell's: late in his life,
now that the failure of the Wittgensteinian philosophies to
fulfil the hopes of their adherents has become impossible to
ignore, he is coming into his own.

Before we leave this subject of past and present misunderstandings one further point is important to make. A
striking feature of the analytic hegemony of recent decades
has been a genuine belief on the part of philosophers holding that the task of philosophy is the elucidation of concepts, and of conceptual schemes, that this is really what all
good philosophers have been doing all along, whether they
realized it or not. Generations of students have acquired
modern techniques of analysis by being taught to use them
on the writings of the great dead; and many books have
been written about the individual giants of the past which
re-present them as having been analytic philosophers of a
kind. As Alasdair MacIntyre has said:[13] 'When British
philosophers do write about the history of philosophy their
method customarily is to treat the historical figure concerned as much like one of their contemporaries as possible
and to debate with him as they would with a colleague at

[11] See *Modern British Philosophy* (ed. Bryan Magee), pp. 131 ff.
[12] In *Modern British Philosophy* (ed. Bryan Magee), p. 88.
[13] In *Modern British Philosophy* (ed. Bryan Magee), p. 193.

the Aristotelian Society'. This has been going on long enough now for the radical yet sincere misunderstanding embodied in much of it to have spread widely both in the contemporary literature and in university teaching. So there is no question of any special injustice being done to Popper when it is said of him that his work is not so very different from that of his distinguished contemporaries, or that the young Popper was not as much at variance with the logical positivists as all that. The attitude has many distinguished victims besides Popper.

4 Popper's Evolutionism and his theory of World 3

The traditional view of scientific method had the following stages in the following order, each giving rise to the next: 1, observation and experiment; 2, inductive generalization; 3, hypothesis; 4, attempted verification of hypothesis; 5, proof or disproof; 6, knowledge. Popper replaced this with: 1, problem (usually rebuff to existing theory or expectation); 2, proposed solution, in other words a new theory; 3, deduction of testable propositions from the new theory; 4, tests, i.e. attempted refutations by, among other things (but only among other things), observation and experiment; 5, preference established between competing theories.

If we ask of Popper's schema: where did the theory or expectation in 1 come from whose breakdown constituted our problem, the short answer usually is: from stage 5 of a prior process. And if we follow successive processes back, we come to expectations that are inborn, not only in human beings but in animals. 'The theory of inborn *ideas* is absurd, I think; but every organism has inborn *reactions* or *responses*; and among them, responses adapted to impending events. These responses we may describe as "expectations" without implying that these "expectations" are conscious. The new-born baby "expects", in this sense, to be fed (and, one could even argue, to be protected and loved). In view of the close relation between expectation and knowledge we may even speak in quite a reasonable sense of "inborn knowledge". This "knowledge" is not, however, *valid a priori*; an inborn expectation, no matter how strong and specific, may be mistaken. (The newborn child may be abandoned, and starve.) Thus we are born with expectations; with "know-

ledge" which, although not *valid a priori*, is *psychologically or genetically a priori*, i.e. prior to all observational
experience.'[1]

So Popper's theory of knowledge is coterminous with a
theory of evolution. Problem-solving is the primal activity:
and the primal problem is survival. 'All *organisms* are constantly, day and night, *engaged in problem-solving*; and so
are all those evolutionary *sequences of organisms* – the
phyla which begin with the most primitive forms and of
which the now living organisms are the latest members.'[2]
In organisms and animals below the human level trial solutions to problems exhibit themselves in the form of new
reactions, new expectations, new modes of behaviour,
which, if they persistently triumph over the trials to which
they are subjected, may eventually modify the creature itself in one of its organs or one of its forms and thus become
(by selection) incorporated in its anatomy. (One reason why
Popper rejects empiricist epistemology, and insists that all
observation must be theory-soaked, is that our sensory
organs themselves, representing as they do sophisticated attempts to adapt to our environment, incorporate theories.)
Error elimination may consist either in so-called natural
selection – which is the failure to survive of an organism
that has failed to make a necessary change, or has made an
inappropriate one – or in the development within the
organism of controls which modify or suppress inappropriate changes.

Like Darwin's, Popper's theory offers no explanation of
the genesis of life but relates only to its development. In
fact Popper believes that origination, whether of life or
theories or works of art, is not susceptible of rational explanation. As he says in different parts of *The Poverty of
Historicism*: 'In the world described by physics nothing
can happen that is truly and intrinsically new. A new

[1] *Conjectures and Refutations*, p. 47.
[2] *Objective Knowledge*, p. 242.

engine may be invented, but we can always analyse it as a re-arrangement of elements which are anything but new. Newness in physics is merely the newness of arrangements or combinations. In direct opposition to this, biological newness is an intrinsic sort of newness.... Novelty cannot be causally or rationally explained, but only intuitively grasped.... So far as newness can be rationally analysed and predicted, it can never be "intrinsic".' The problem of emergence, the emergence of the genuinely new, preoccupies him and is one of the subjects on which there may be important contributions from him still to come.

In the biological process of evolution, seen as the history of problem-solving, one development is of an importance above all others, and that is the development of language. Animals make noises with expressive and signalling functions, but to these two purposes, virtually always present in human speech, man has added at least two more, the descriptive and the argumentative functions (though the most sophisticated forms of animal communication, like the dance of the bees, already include some very rudimentary descriptive messages). Language made possible, among so many other things, the formulation of descriptions of the world, and thus made understanding possible. It gave rise to the concepts of truth and falsity. In short it made the development of reason possible – or rather was itself a part of the development of reason – and thus marked the emergence of man from the animal kingdom. (Incidentally the fact that man emerged from the animal kingdom by slow degrees in the way he did means that he was living in groups for a huge span of time through the process, so the widely held view that all social phenomena can ultimately be explained in terms of human nature must be wrong: man was social for a long time before he was human.) Popper believes that it is language, in the sense of a structured form of contact, communication, description and argument through signs and symbols, that makes us human not only as a species but as individuals: that for each one of us the acquisition of a language in this sense makes full human consciousness, the consciousness of self, possible. (In a striking number of ways Popper's work in this field anticipated that of Chomsky.)

The first descriptions of the world seem to have been animistic, superstitious, magical; and to question them or anything else that gave cohesion and identity to a tribe was tabu and usually met with death. So the individual primitive man came into a world dominated by abstractions – kinship relations, forms of social organisation and government, law, custom, convention, tradition, alliances and enmities, ritual, religion, myth, superstition, language – all of which were manmade but none of them made by *him*, and most of them not amenable to alteration by him either, or even open to questioning by him. As against each man, then, they stood as a kind of objective reality, shaping him from birth, making him human, determining almost everything about his life, yet quasi-autonomous. It is Popper's contention that most such things were never planned or intended. 'How does an animal path in the jungle arise? Some animal may break through the undergrowth in order to get to a drinking-place. Other animals find it easiest to use the same track. Thus it may be widened and improved by use. It is not planned – it is an unintended consequence of the need for easy or swift movement. This is how a path is originally made – perhaps even by men – and how language and any other institutions which are useful may arise, and how they may owe their existence and development to their usefulness. They are not planned or intended, and there was perhaps no need for them before they came into existence. But they may create a new need, or a new set of aims: the aim-structure of animals or men is not "given", but it develops, with the help of some kind of feedback mechanism, out of earlier aims, and out of results which were or were not aimed at. In this way, a whole new universe of possibilities or potentialities may arise: a world which is to a large extent *autonomous*.'[3]

Throughout his account of the evolution of life and the emergence of man and the development of civilization, Popper makes use of the notion not only of an objective world of material things (which he calls 'World 1') and a subjective world of minds (World 2) but of a third world, a world of objective structures which are the products, not necessarily intentional, of minds or living creatures; but which, once produced, exist independently of them. Forerunners of this in the animal world are nests built by birds or ants or wasps, honeycombs, spiders' webs, beavers' dams, all of which are highly complicated structures built by the animal outside its own body in order to solve its problems. The structures themselves become the most centrally important part of the animal's environment, towards which much of its most important behaviour is oriented – indeed, it is commonly born in one of them, which in that case constitutes its very first experience of the physical environment outside its mother's body. Furthermore, some of the animal kingdom's structures are abstract: forms of social organization, for instance, and patterns of communication. In man, some of the biological characteristics which developed to cope with the environment changed that environment in the most spectacular ways: the human hand is only one example. And man's abstract structures have at all times equalled in scale and degree of elaboration his transformation of the physical environment: language, ethics, law, religion, philosophy, the sciences, the arts, institutions. Like those of animals, only more so, his creations acquired a central importance in the environment to which he had then to adapt himself, and which therefore shaped him. Their objective existence in relation to him meant that he could examine them, evaluate and criticize them, explore, extend, revise or revolutionize them, and indeed

[3] *Objective Knowledge*, pp. 117–118.

make wholly unexpected discoveries within them. And this is true of his most abstract creations of all, for example mathematics. 'I agree with Brouwer that the sequence of natural numbers is a human construction. But although we create this sequence, it creates its own autonomous problems in its turn. The distinction between odd and even numbers is not created by us: it is an unintended and unavoidable consequence of our creation. Prime numbers, of course, are simply unintended autonomous and objective facts; and in their case it is obvious that there are many facts here for us to *discover*: there are conjectures like Goldbach's.[4] And these conjectures, though they refer indirectly to objects of our creation, refer directly to problems and facts which have somehow emerged from our creation and which we cannot control or influence: they are hard facts, and the truth about them is often hard to discover. This exemplifies what I mean when I say that the third world is largely autonomous, though created by us.'[5]

World 3, then, is the world of ideas, art, science, language, ethics, institutions – the whole cultural heritage, in short – in so far as this is encoded and preserved in such World 1 objects as brains, books, machines, films, computers, pictures, and records of every kind. Although all World 3 entities are products of human minds, they may exist independently of any knowing subject – the Linear B scripts of the Minoan civilization have only recently been deciphered – provided they are encoded and preserved in some potentially accessible World 1 form. (Hence the crucial difference between the knowledge in people's heads and the knowledge in libraries, the latter being far and away the more important.) In *Facing Reality* (p. 170) Sir John Eccles subscribes to the conclusions 'that man alone has a proposi-

[4] Goldbach conjectured that every even number is the sum of two primes. No one has yet found a proof for this, yet it fits every known case it has been applied to. – B.M.

[5] *Objective Knowledge*, p. 118.

tional language and that this language can be employed only by subjects who have conceptual thought, which is essentially thought related to the components of World 3. This thought transcends the perceptual present.... By contrast the behaviour of animals is derived from their perceptual present and their background conditioning.... There is no evidence that animals share this World even in the smallest degree. In this fundamental respect men are radically different in kind from animals.'

The concept of a manmade yet autonomous third world is one of the most promising growth points of Popper's philosophy. Its application to the body-mind problem is the subject of one of his unpublished books. (The view that it is through interaction with World 3 that we become selves is alone endless in its ramifications.) Quite apart from this, the World 3 theory helps us to see why both sides in the age-old dispute about whether moral, aesthetic and other standards are objective or subjective have put forward unanswerable arguments. It offers an analysis of another problem central to Western philosophy, the problem of social change: for it is because of the objective character of man's third-world creations, and the transactions to which this gives rise between him and them, that they – ideas, institutions, languages, ethics, arts, sciences and all the other things I listed before – have histories. They do not necessarily progress, but they are of their nature open to change, and for most of the time they change continuously. Above all, Popper's theory explains how an evolutionary process can have a rationale without there being (as, say, Marx believed) any overall plan or plot, and also without there being (as, say, Hegel believed) some spirit or vital force moving the process along, as it were, from inside. This is an extraordinarily illuminating idea, likely to prove most rich in its applications. Ernst Gombrich's highly original use of it in the history and criticism of art has resulted in work which is regarded by many as having a touch of genius. As for Popper's own use of it : especially important are the solutions he offers along these lines to problems about political change which have engrossed the greatest political philosophers from Plato to Marx; and to problems about intellectual and artistic change which have engrossed many philosophers since Hegel, and some long before.

In the history of World 3 as a whole the most important development since the emergence of language has been the emergence of criticism, and later of the acceptability of criticism. As I said earlier, all or almost all human societies of which we have knowledge seem to have had an interpretation of the world which was articulated in some myth or religion, and in primitive societies any questioning of its truth is usually punishable by death. The truth is to be kept inviolate, and handed on unsullied from generation to generation. For this purpose institutions develop – mysteries, priesthoods, and, at an advanced stage, schools. 'A school of this kind never admits a new idea. New ideas are heresies, and lead to schisms; should a member of the school try to change the doctrine, then he is expelled as a heretic. But the heretic claims, as a rule, that his is the true doctrine of the founder. Thus not even the inventor admits that he has introduced an invention; he believes, rather, that he is returning to the true orthodoxy which has somehow been perverted.'[6]

Popper believes that as a matter of history the first schools to not only permit criticism but encourage and welcome it were those of the pre-Socratic philosophers of ancient Greece, starting with Thales and his pupil Anaximander and *his* pupil Anaximenes.[7] This spelt the end of the dogmatic tradition of passing on an unsullied truth, and the beginning of a new rational tradition of subjecting speculations to critical discussion. It was the inauguration of scientific method. Error was turned from disaster to ad-

[6] *Conjectures and Refutations*, p. 149.
[7] See also the quotation from Xenophanes on p. 28.

vantage. For dogmatic man, like animals and the lower organisms, had stood or fallen with his theories. 'On the pre-scientific level, we are often ourselves destroyed, eliminated, with our false theories; we perish with our false theories. On the scientific level, we systematically try to eliminate our false theories – we try to let our false theories die in our stead.'[8] When man no longer shared the death of his theories he was emboldened to venture. Whereas, before, the entire weight of intellectual tradition had been defensive and had served to preserve existing doctrines, now, for the first time, it was put behind a questioning attitude and became a force for change. The pre-Socratics concerned themselves with questions about the natural world. Socrates applied the same critical rationality to human behaviour and social institutions. There began that runaway growth of enquiry and resultant knowledge which almost sensationally differentiates the civilization of ancient Greece, and its legatees, from all others.

[8] Popper in *Modern British Philosophy* (ed. Bryan Magee), p. 73.

5 Objective Knowledge

A seamless unfolding of the story from the amoeba to Einstein exhibits the same pattern throughout its length. 'The tentative solutions which animals and plants incorporate into their anatomy and their behaviour are biological analogues of theories; and vice versa : theories correspond (as do many exosomatic products such as honeycombs, and especially exosomatic tools, such as spiders' webs) to endosomatic organs and their ways of functioning. Just like theories, organs and their functions are tentative adaptations to the world we live in. And just like theories, or like tools, new organs and their functions, and also new kinds of behaviour, exert their influence on the first world which they may help to change.'[1] Popper has characterized the underlying pattern of this continuous development in the formula

$$P_1 \rightarrow TS \rightarrow EE \rightarrow P_2$$

where P_1 is the inital problem, TS the trial solution proposed, EE the process of error elimination applied to the trial solution and P_2 the resulting situation, with new problems. It is essentially a feedback process. It is not cyclic, for P_2 is always different from P_1 : even complete failure to solve a problem teaches us something new about where its difficulties lie, and what the minimum conditions are which any solution for it must meet – and therefore alters the problem situation. Nor is it dialectical (in any Hegelian or Marxist sense) since it regards contradiction (as distinct from criticism) as something that cannot be accommodated

[1] *Objective Knowledge*, p. 145.

on any level, and still less welcomed.

This formula incorporates some of the most important of Popper's ideas. He himself has put a good strong saddle on it and ridden it into many different fields of human enquiry; and where he has not been, some follower of his often has. For most of his life he maintained that it was not applicable to mathematics or logic. He was belatedly convinced that it was by the work of Imre Lakatos – who was thus in this respect more Popperian than Popper. About the arts Popper has published little, though music in particular means a great deal to him, and it was in connection with his early studies in the history of music that his seminal idea about problem-solving came to him. However, in Ernst Gombrich's *Art and Illusion* the history of the visual arts is accounted for in specifically Popperian terms of an endless and 'gradual modification of the traditional schematic conventions of image making under the pressure of novel demands'. Virtually all processes of organic development (whether literal or figurative) and all learning process can be looked at in this way, even the process by which human beings get to know each other. The psychiatrist Anthony Storr, without having read Popper, arrived at the following conclusion: 'When we enter a new situation in life and are confronted by a new person, we bring with us the prejudices of the past and our previous experiences of people. These prejudices we project upon the new person. Indeed, getting to know a person is largely a matter of withdrawing projections; of dispelling the smoke-screen of what we imagine he is like and replacing it with the reality of what he is actually like.'[2]

The adoption of this approach has certain natural consequences. First of all it focuses interest on *problems*, not only for oneself but in one's appreciation of the efforts of others. A task does not begin with the attempt to solve a problem (the trial solution is the second term in the formu-

[2] *The Observer Magazine*, 12 July, 1970.

la, not the first). It begins with the problem itself, and with the reasons for its being a problem. One learns to work hard and long at the formulation of *problems* before one switches one's main attention to the search for possible solutions; and one's degree of success in the latter is often determined by one's degree of success in the former. If one studies the work of, say, a philosopher, the first question one asks oneself is : 'What problem is he trying to solve?' This may sound obvious, but in my experience most students of philosophy are not taught to ask, and do not think to ask themselves, this question. Rather they ask : 'What is he trying to say?' As a result they commonly have the experience of thinking they understand what he is saying without seeing the point of his saying it. For only by understanding his problem-situation could they do that.

Another consequence, which is fundamental to Popper's whole philosophy and is likely to affect the way someone influenced by it sees everything, is the realization that complex structures – whether intellectual, artistic, social, administrative or whatever – are only to be created and changed by stages, through a critical feedback process of successive adjustments. The notion that they can be created, or made over, at a stroke, as if from a blueprint, is an illusion which can never be actualized. Among other things, this evolutionary view leads one inevitably to a concern with developments over time. For instance the history of science, or philosophy, is seen not as a record of past errors but as a running argument, a chain of linked problems and their tentative solutions, with us in the present walking forward, if we are lucky, holding one end. Whereas positivist and linguistic philosophers have been, on the whole, notoriously little concerned with the history of their own subject, a Popperian approach leads to a sense of personal involvement in the history of ideas. (Hence the fact that Popper himself, a philosopher of science familiar with modern physics, is also a passionate scholar.)

A consequence of always proceeding from problems which really are problems – problems which one actually *has*, and has grappled with – is, for oneself, that one will be existentially committed to one's work; and for the work itself, that it will have what Existentialists call 'authenticity'. It will be not only an intellectual interest but an emotional involvement, the meeting of a felt human need. Another consequence will be an unconcern for conventional distinctions between subjects : all that matters is that one should have an interesting problem and be genuinely trying to solve it.

Popper's philosophy – objectively regarded and not confused with the conduct of any individual, even of Popper himself – could scarcely be more undogmatic, for it puts the greatest premium of all on boldness of imagination; and it holds that we never actually *know* – that our approach to any and every situation or problem needs to be always such as to accommodate not merely unforeseeable contributions but the permanent possibility of a radical transformation of the whole conceptual scheme with which, and even within which, we are operating. It is fundamentally at variance with all views of science or rationality which see these as excluding passion or imagination or creative intuition; and it condemns as 'scientism' the notion that science gives us certain knowledge and might even be able one day to give us settled answers to all our legitimate questions. A great deal of the disillusionment with science and reason which is so widespread in our age is based on precisely such mistaken notions of what science and reason are – and to that extent does not apply to Popperism. If Popper is right, there are not two cultures – one scientific and the other aesthetic, or one rational and the other irrational – but one. The scientist and the artist, far from being engaged in opposed or incompatible activities, are both trying to extend our understanding of experience by the use of creative imagination subjected to critical control, and so both are using irrational as well as rational faculties. Both are exploring the unknown and trying to articulate the search and its findings. Both are seekers after truth who make indispensable use of intuition.

But it follows that if learning and growth and development proceed through the submission of expectations to the test of experience, and the acknowledgement of areas of conflict, and the turning of these to progressive use (or, even, on the purely intellectual level, through the control and correction of speculations, which may be more or less bold, by criticism, which may be more or less severe) then we can never make an absolutely fresh start. Even if it were possible for a man to begin from the beginning he would get, by the time he died, no further than Neanderthal man. These are facts which many people of a radical or independent turn of mind are intensely reluctant to face. Before we as individuals are even conscious of our existence we have been profoundly influenced for a considerable time (since before birth) by our relationship to other individuals who have complicated histories, and are members of a society which has an infinitely more complicated and longer history than they do (and are members of it at a particular time and place in that history); and by the time we are able to make conscious choices we are already making use of categories in a language which has reached a particular degree of development through the lives of countless generations of human beings before us. Popper does not say, though he might have done, that our very existence itself is the direct result of a social act performed by two other people whom we are powerless to choose or prevent, and whose genetic legacy is built into our body and personality. We are social creatures to the inmost centre of our being. The notion that one can begin anything at all from scratch, free from the past, or unindebted to others, could not conceivably be more wrong.

This truth extends to intellectual and artistic activities of every kind. The very possibility of making marks on a surface, or producing noises, in order to express or communicate or give pleasure, was reached only after countless evolutionary ages; and artists who imagine they are going back to the beginning are, whatever they do, taking things up at a highly advanced stage and standing on the shoulders of innumerable generations. In everything we are, and everything we do, we inherit the *whole* past, and however much we might want to make ourselves independent of it there is no way in which we possibly can. This gives tradition an inescapable importance. It is where we have to start from, if only by reacting against it. Usually the way we make advances is by criticizing it and effecting changes: we *use* the tradition, we ride forward on its back. The situation is fundamentally the same in the sciences as in the arts. 'All this means that a young scientist who hopes to make discoveries is badly advised if his teacher tells him, "Go round and observe," and that he is well advised if his teacher tells him: "Try to learn what people are discussing nowadays in science. Find out where difficulties arise, and take an interest in disagreements. These are the questions which you should take up." In other words, you should study the *problem situation* of the day. This means that you pick up, and try to continue, a line of enquiry which has the whole background of the earlier development of science behind it; you fall in with the tradition of science.... From the point of view of what we want as scientists – understanding, prediction, analysis, and so on – the world in which we live is extremely complex. I should be tempted to say that it is infinitely complex, if the phrase had any meaning. We do not know where or how to start our analysis of this world. There is no wisdom to tell us. Even the scientific tradition does not tell us. It only tells us where and how other people started and where they got to.'[3]

Since the fact that things have reached this or that point

[3] *Conjectures and Refutations*, p. 129.

in this or that branch of this or that science, or academic field, or art (or society, or language) is an objective fact as far as each individual is concerned when he comes on the scene; and since any criticism he may put forward, or proposed change, or solution to a problem, has to be formulated in language before it can be tested or ·even discussed; any such proposal becomes an *objective* proposal. It can be argued about, attacked, defended, used, without reference to the man who put it forward. Indeed, this is what happens most of the time with interesting ideas. This underlines the enormous importance of objectifying our ideas in language or behaviour or works of art. While they are only in our heads they are barely criticizable. Their public formulation itself usually leads to progress. And the validity of any argument about them is again an objective matter: it is not determined by how many individuals are prepared to accept it. Even if a theory is a scientific one and has been most rigorously tested by its proposer, the scientific world does not adopt it until his experiments and observations have been repeated by others. 'I know', considered as a statement about me, asserts my disposition to do and say and believe certain things, and also claims justification for this; but none of that is knowledge in the objective sense: no one is going to accord my untested assertions the status of knowledge (unless the knowledge is of something in my own states of consciousness, as when I answer the questions of the optician, or tell the doctor where the pain is – and even these direct reports of our own current states of awareness are not always accurate, as every doctor discovers from experience). Thus in scientific work we do not take even our own observations as certain, indeed we do not even accept them as scientific observations, until we have repeated and tested them. In all these respects, then, knowledge is objective. It inhabits the public domain (World 3). It is not in the private states of mind of individuals (World 2).

In this private, individual sense most human knowledge is not 'known' by anybody at all. It exists only on paper. The desk on which I write is surrounded by shelves of reference books : let us take one which Popper has himself used for this example – a book of logarithm tables. These constitute knowledge of a prodigiously useful kind which is in active use every day all over the world in the construction of buildings, bridges, roads, aeroplanes, machines and a thousand other things. Yet I doubt whether there is a soul in the world who 'knows' these tables, not even the man who compiled my book of them (indeed, it may even have been compiled by computer). This goes for records of every kind. Even an individual scholar devoting his life to creating his own works of scholarship normally makes notes, usually copious, from all sorts of documents, books, works of reference and so on, and writes his books from his notes : he does not even 'know' (in the World 2 sense) everything in his own books. He cannot reel off all the statistical and other tables, dates, page references and so on; he cannot recite all the quotations word for word – indeed, the whole point is *he cannot recite his own books*. They are on paper : they are not in his head. The libraries and record systems and filing cabinets of the world consist of World 3 material most of which is likewise not in anybody's head but is nevertheless knowledge of a more or less valuable and useful kind. Indeed, it is most of the knowledge we have. Its status as knowledge and its value and usefulness are independent of whether there is anyone who 'knows' it in the subjective sense. Knowledge in the objective sense is knowledge without a knower : it is knowledge without a knowing subject.

From this standpoint Popper launches an onslaught on orthodox epistemology. 'Traditional epistemology has studied knowledge or thought in a subjective sense – in the sense of the ordinary usage of the words "I know" or "I am thinking". This, I assert, has led students of epistemology into irrelevancies : while intending to study scientific knowledge, they studied in fact something which is of no relevance to scientific knowledge. For *scientific knowledge* simply is not knowledge in the sense of the ordinary usage of the words "I know". . . . the traditional epistemology, of Locke, Berkeley, Hume, and even of Russell, is irrelevant, in a pretty strict sense of the word. It is a corollary of this thesis that a large part of contemporary epistemology is irrelevant also. This includes modern epistemic logic, *if* we assume that it aims at a theory of *scientific knowledge*. However, any epistemic logician can easily make himself completely immune from my criticism, simply by making clear that he does not aim at contributing to the *theory of scientific knowledge*.'[4]

As Popper says in the Preface to *Objective Knowledge*: 'The essays in this book break with a tradition that can be traced back to Aristotle – the tradition of this commonsense theory of knowledge. I am a great admirer of common sense which, I assert, is essentially self-critical. But while I am prepared to uphold to the last the essential truth of *commonsense realism*, I regard the *commonsense theory of knowledge* as a subjectivist blunder. This blunder has dominated Western philosophy. I have made an attempt to eradicate it, and to replace it by an objective theory of essentially conjectural knowledge. This may be a bold claim but I do not apologize for it.'

[4] *Objective Knowledge*, p. 108.

6   The Open Society

From Plato to Marx most great political philosophies have had their roots in related views not only of social and historical development but of logic and science, and ultimately of epistemology. Readers who have followed me thus far can see now that Popper's is no exception. Because he regards living as first and foremost a process of problem-solving he wants societies which are conducive to problem-solving. And because problem-solving calls for the bold propounding of trial solutions which are then subjected to criticism and error-elimination, he wants forms of society which permit of the untrammelled assertion of differing proposals, followed by criticism, followed by the genuine possibility of change in the light of criticism. Regardless of any moral considerations (and it is of the highest importance to grasp this) he believes that a society organized on such lines will be more effective at solving its problems, and therefore more successful in achieving the aims of its members, than if it were organized on other lines. The common notion that the most efficient form of society, in theory at least, would be some form of dictatorship, is on this view utterly mistaken. That the dozen or more countries in the world that have the highest living standards (not that this would be his main criterion) are all liberal democracies is not because democracy is a luxury which their wealth enables them to afford: on the contrary, the mass of their people were living in poverty when they achieved universal suffrage. The causal connection is the other way round. Democracy has played a vital role in bringing about and sustaining high living standards. Materially, as in other ways, a society is practically bound to be more successful if it has free institutions than if it does not.

All government policies, indeed all executive and administrative decisions, involve empirical predictions : 'If we do X, Y will follow : on the other hand if we want to achieve B we must do A.' As everyone knows, such predictions not infrequently turn out to be wrong – everyone makes mistakes – and it is *normal* for them to have to be modified as their application proceeds. A policy is a hypothesis which has to be tested against reality and corrected in the light of experience. Detecting mistakes and inherent dangers by critical examination and discussion beforehand is an altogether more rational procedure, and one as a rule less wasteful of resources, people and time, than waiting till they reveal themselves in practice. Furthermore it is often only by critical examination of the practical results, as distinct from the policies themselves, that some of the mistakes are to be identified. For, in this connexion, it is essential to face the fact that any action we take is likely to have unintended consequences. This simple point is one whose implications are highly charged for politics, administration and any form of planning. It can be illustrated easily. If I want to buy a house my very appearance in the market as a buyer will tend to raise the price; but although this is a direct consequence of my action no one can possibly maintain that it is an intended one. And when I go on to take out an insurance policy to raise a mortgage, this will tend to raise the value of the insurance company's shares; and again this direct consequence of my action has no connection with my intentions. (See pp. 103 and 105.) Things are all the time happening which nobody planned or wants. And this inescapable fact should be allowed for both in decision making and in the creation of organizational structures : if it is not it will be a permanent source of distortion. This again reinforces the need for critical vigilance in the administration of policies, and the allowance for their correction by error elimination. So not only do authorities which forbid prior critical examination of their policies condemn themselves to making many of their mistakes in a more expensive form, and discovering them later, than they need; they also – if, as is usually the case, they likewise forbid critical examination of the practical application of their policies – condemn themselves to pressing on with mistakes for some time after these have begun to produce injurious unintended consequences. The whole approach, characteristic of highly authoritarian structures, is anti-rational. As a result the more rigid perish with their false theories, or at best (if they are lucky and ruthless) ossify, and the less rigid make a progress which is bruised, costly and unnecessarily slow.

It is not enough for anyone with power (whether in government or some lesser organization) to have policies, in the sense of aims and goals, however clearly formulated. There must also be the means for achieving them. If the means do not exist, they must be created : otherwise the goals, however good, will not be reached. In one respect, therefore, organizations and institutions of every kind have to be looked on as machines for implementing policies. And it is as difficult to design an organization so that its output is what you want as it is a physical machine. If an engineer designs a new machine but his design is not right for the purpose; or if he is adapting an already existing machine, but has not changed it in all necessary ways; then what will come out of it can not possibly be what he wants : it can be only what the machine can produce – which will not only be something other than what he wants but may be seriously defective by any standards, and even dangerous. And precisely this is true of a great deal of organizational machinery : it is incapable of doing what the people operating it require of it, regardless of their cleverness, good intentions or well-formulated goals. There is need, therefore, for a political (or administrative) technology as well as a political (or administrative) science, one that embodies a permanently but constructively critical attitude to organizational means in the light of changing goals. The implementation of every policy needs to be tested: and this is to be done not by looking for evidence that one's efforts are having the desired effects but by looking for evidence that they are not. Testing in this sense is usually cheap and easy in practice, if only because minute accuracy is seldom necessary. The British higher education system already contains at least one department devoted to the Popperian study of institutions (set up by Tyrrell Burgess at the North East London Polytechnic) and its results are both simple and of great potential usefulness, for huge sums and efforts are commonly expended on mistaken policies without any provision for the tiny sums and efforts required at the same time to see if undesired results are emerging. People in organizations tend, on the contrary, to turn a blind eye to evidence that what they want is not happening, in spite of the fact that such evidence is precisely what they ought to be looking for. And of course the perpetual search for, and admission of, error at even the organizational level is hardest of all in authoritarian structures. Thereby does their irrationality extend into the very instruments they use.

Popper's moral sentiments about political matters have been expressed, if with less depth of passion, by others. His writing is deeply moving at this level; but what is distinctive about him is the wealth and power of argumentation with which he has shown that the heart has reason on its side. For it has been widely believed, and in our century more than any other, that rationality, logic, the scientific approach, call for a society which is centrally organized, and planned and ordered as a whole. Popper has shown that this, besides being authoritarian, rests on a mistaken and superseded conception of science. Rationality, logic and a scientific approach all point to a society which is 'open' and pluralistic, within which incompatible views are expressed and conflicting aims pursued; a society in which everyone is free to investigate problem-situations and to propose solutions; a society in which everyone is free to criticize the proposed solutions of others, most importantly those of the government, whether in prospect or application; and above all a society in which the government's policies are changed in the light of criticism.

Since policies are normally advocated, and their implementation supervised, by people who are in some way or other committed to them, changes of more than a certain magnitude involve changes in personnel. So if the open society is to be a reality the most fundamental requirement is that those in power should be removable, at reasonable intervals and without violence, and replaceable by others with different policies. And for this to be a genuine option people with policies different from those of the government must be free to constitute themselves as an alternative government, ready to take over: that is to say they must be able to organize, speak, write, publish, broadcast and teach in criticism of the people in power, and must have constitutionally guaranteed access to a means of replacing them, for example by regularly held free elections.

Such a society is what Popper means by 'democracy', though as always he would set no special store by the word. The point to be emphasized is that he sees democracy in terms of the preservation of certain kinds of institution – what used to be called, before American cold war propaganda brought the term into disrepute, free institutions – especially those which enable the ruled effectively to criticize their rulers and to change them without bloodshed. He does not see it as just the election of governments by a majority of the governed, for that view leads to what he calls 'the paradox of democracy'. What if the majority votes for a party, such as a Fascist or Communist party, which does not believe in free institutions and nearly always destroys them when it gets into power? The man committed to choice of government by majority vote is here in an insoluble dilemma : any attempt to stop the Fascist or Communist party taking over means acting contrary to his principles, yet if they do take over they will put an end to democracy. Furthermore he has no moral basis for active resistance to, say, a Nazi regime if a majority has voted for it, as in Germany it very nearly did. Popper's approach is free of this paradox. A man committed to the preservation of free institutions can without self-contradiction defend them against attack from any direction, whether from minorities or majorities. And if there is an attempt to overthrow free institutions by armed violence he can without self-contradiction defend them by armed violence; for if, in a society whose government can be changed without force, a group nevertheless resorts to it because it can not get its way otherwise, then whatever it may think or intend it is setting up by violence a government which will be removable only by violence – in other words a tyranny. Indeed, force may be morally justified against an existing regime which sustains itself by force, if one's aim is to establish free institutions – and one has a serious chance of succeeding – for then one's object is to replace the rule of violence by a rule of reason and tolerance.

Popper points to other paradoxes which his approach avoids. One already suggested is the paradox of tolerance : if a society extends unlimited tolerance it is likely to be destroyed, and tolerance with it. So a tolerant society must be prepared in some circumstances to suppress the enemies of tolerance. It should not of course do so unless they constitute a genuine danger – quite apart from anything else this leads to witch-hunting. And it should try all in its power to meet such people first on the level of rational argument. But they may 'begin by denouncing all argument; they may forbid their followers to listen to rational argument, because it is deceptive, and teach them to answer arguments by the use of their fists or pistols'; and a tolerant society can survive only if it is prepared, in the last analysis, to restrain such people by force. 'We should ... consider incitement to intolerance and persecution as criminal, in the same way as we should consider incitement to murder, or to kidnapping, or to the revival of the slave trade, as criminal.'[1]

Another, more familiar paradox, first implicitly formulated by Plato, is the paradox of freedom. Unqualified freedom, like unqualified tolerance, is not only self-destructive but bound to produce its opposite – for if all restraints were removed there would be nothing whatever to stop the strong enslaving the weak (or meek). So complete freedom would bring about the end of freedom, and therefore proponents of complete freedom are in actuality, whatever their intentions, enemies of freedom. Popper points more particularly to the paradox of economic freedom, which makes possible the unrestrained exploitation of the poor by the rich, and results in the almost complete loss of economic freedom by the poor. Here again there 'must be a *political* remedy – a remedy similar to the one which we use against physical violence. We must construct social institutions, enforced by the power of the state, for the protection of the economically weak from the economically strong.... This, of course, means that the principle of non-intervention, of an unrestrained economic system, has to be given up; if we wish freedom to be safeguarded, then we must demand that the policy of unlimited economic freedom be replaced by the planned economic intervention of the state. We must demand that unrestrained *capitalism* give way to an *economic interventionism*.'[2] And he goes on to point out that opponents of state interventionism as such are guilty of self-contradiction. 'Which freedom should the state protect? The freedom of the labour market, or the freedom of the poor to unite? Whichever decision is

[1] *The Open Society and Its Enemies*, vol. i, p. 265.
[2] *The Open Society and Its Enemies*, vol. ii, p. 125.

taken, it leads to state intervention, to the use of organized political power, of the state as well as of unions, in the field of economic conditions. It leads, under all circumstances, to an extension of the economic responsibility of the state, whether or not this responsibility is consciously accepted.'[3] And more generally : 'If the state does not interfere, then other semi-political organizations such as monopolies, trusts, unions, etc., may interfere, reducing the freedom of the market to a fiction. On the other hand, it is most important to realize that without a carefully protected free market, the whole economic system must cease to serve its only rational purpose, that is, *to satisfy the demands of the consumer....* Economic "planning" that does not plan for economic freedom in this sense will lead dangerously close to totalitarianism.'[4]

In all these cases the maximum possible tolerance or freedom is an optimum, not an absolute, for it has to be restricted if it is to exist at all. The government intervention which alone can guarantee it is a dangerous weapon : without it, or with too little, freedom dies; but with too much of it freedom dies also. We are brought back to the inescapability of control – which must mean, if it is to be effective, removability – of government by the governed as the *sine qua non* of democracy. This however, though necessary, is not sufficient. It does not guarantee the preservation of freedom, for nothing can : the price of freedom is eternal vigilance. As Popper has remarked, institutions are like fortresses in that although to be effective they have to be properly constructed this alone will not make them work : they have also to be properly manned.

By and large political philosophers have regarded the most important question as being 'Who should rule?' and their differing philosophies seek to justify different answers : a single man, the well-born, the rich, the wise, the

[3] *The Open Society and Its Enemies*, vol. ii, p. 179.
[4] *The Open Society and Its Enemies*, vol. ii, p. 348.

strong, the good, the majority, the proletariat, and so on.
But the question itself is mistaken, for several reasons. First,
it leads straight to another of Popper's paradoxes, which he
calls 'the paradox of sovereignty'. If, say, power is put in
the hands of the wisest man, he may from the depths of his
wisdom adjudge : 'Not I but the morally good should be
the ruler'. If the morally good has power he may say, being
saintly : 'It is wrong for me to impose my will on others.
Not I but the majority should rule'. The majority, having
power, may say : 'We want a strong man to impose order
and tell us what to do'. A second objection is that the question : 'Where should sovereignty lie?' rests on the assumption that ultimate power must be somewhere, which is not
the case. In most societies there are different and to some
extent conflicting power centres, not one of which can get
everything its own way. In some societies power is quite
widely diffused. The question 'Yes, but where does it *ultimately* lie?' eliminates before it is raised the possibility of
control over rulers, when this is the most important of all
things to establish. The vital question is not 'Who should
rule?' but 'How can we minimize misrule – both the likeli-
hood of its occurring and, when it does occur, its consequences?'

The argument up to this point, then, is that the best
society we can have, from a practical as well as moral
point of view, is one which extends the maximum possible
freedom to its members; that the maximum freedom is a
qualified one; that it can be created and sustained at optimum level only by institutions designed for that purpose
and backed by the power of the state; that this involves
large-scale state intervention in political, economic and
social life; that too little or too much intervention will alike
result in unnecessary encroachments on freedom; that the
best way to minimize the dangers both ways is to preserve,
as the most important institutions of all, constitutional
means whereby the governed can remove the wielders of

state power and put in their places other men with different policies; that any attempt to render such institutions ineffective is an attempt to introduce authoritarian government and should be prevented, if necessary by force; that the use of force against tyranny may be justified even when the tyranny has majority support; but that the only untyrannical aims the use of force can have are the defence of free institutions where they exist and their establishment where they do not.

It has always seemed to me obvious that this is a philosophy of social democracy – as plainly anti-conservative on the one side as it is anti-totalitarian (and as such anti-Communist) on the other. For it is above all else a philosophy of how to change things, and to do so in a way which, unlike violent revolution, is rational and humane. As I believe I have now shown, it is seamlessly interwoven with Popper's philosophy of science. But we must also remember that the man who wrote *The Open Society* had, just behind him, 20 years of involvement with active members of the Social Democratic Party of Austria. As a Social Democrat he had become convinced that the nationalization of the means of production, distribution and exchange, which constituted the foundations of his party's platform, would not of itself solve the problems it was intended to solve yet might well destroy the values the party held most dear. Being a young man, without political influence except on his friends, what he would have liked to see but assumed he had no chance of seeing was the renunciation by the Social Democrats of the Marxist analysis of social change, and the replacement of this by the sort of ideas he was arguing for. In the end he became disillusioned with his party, not primarily because of its muddle-headedness intellectually but because of the way it exposed the workers to violence which it had no programme for resisting; because of its leaders' fear of responsibility; and above all because of its complicity with the Communists in not offering all-out resistance to the Nazis' seizure of power – even though its motives were not, like the Communists', machiavellian, but characteristically flabby. He has retained ever since a distrust of Social Democratic parties. He would now describe himself, if pressed, as a liberal in the old fashioned sense of that word.

And here I must declare an interest. I am a democratic socialist and I believe that the young Popper worked out, as no one else has ever done, what the philosophical foundations of democratic socialism should be. And like him I would like to see these ideas replace the garbled mixture of Marxism and liberal-minded opportunism which passes for political theory on the democratic left : in 1962 I published a book advocating this in the context of British Labour Party politics called *The New Radicalism*. In short, while making it clear that Popper is no longer a socialist, I want to claim his ideas for the democratic socialism in which he was so deeply enmeshed when he began to produce them, and in response to whose needs they were produced. This is where I believe their real significance is, and where their future lies. My longest-running argument with the older Popper is about what in my contention is his failure to accept, in matters of practical politics, the radical consequences of his own ideas. (If I am right about this, there is at least one famous precedent : Marx used to protest, in later life, that he was not a Marxist.)

The general guiding principle for public policy put forward in *The Open Society* is : 'Minimize avoidable suffering'. Characteristically, this has the immediate effect of drawing attention to *problems*. If, say, an Education Authority set itself the aim of maximizing opportunity for the children under its care it might, understandably, not be sure how to go about doing this; or it might start thinking in terms of spending its money on the building of model schools. But if, rather, it sets itself the aim of *minimizing disadvantage*, this directs its attention immediately to the most underprovided schools – those with the worst staffing problems, the most overcrowded classes, the slummiest buildings, the least or worst educational equipment – and makes doing something about *them* the first priority. The Popperian approach has this consequence right across the board: instead of encouraging one to think about building Utopia it makes one seek out, and try to remove, the specific social evils under which human beings are suffering. In this way it is above all a practical approach, and yet one devoted to change. It starts from concern with human beings, and involves a permanent, active willingness to remould institutions.

'Minimize unhappiness' is not just a negative formulation of the Utilitarian maxim 'Maximize happiness'. There is a logical asymmetry here: we do not know how to make people happy, but we do know ways of lessening their unhappiness. Readers will at once see an analogy between this and the verifiability or falsifiability of scientific statements. 'I believe that there is, from the ethical point of view, no symmetry between suffering and happiness, or between pain and pleasure.... human suffering makes a direct moral appeal, namely, the appeal for help, while there is no similar call to increase the happiness of a man who is doing well anyway. (A further criticism of the Utilitarian formula "Maximize pleasure" is that it assumes, in principle, a continuous pleasure-pain scale which allows us to treat degrees of pain as negative degrees of pleasure. But, from the moral point of view, pain cannot be outweighed by pleasure, and especially not one man's pain by another man's pleasure. Instead of the greatest happiness for the greatest number, one should demand, more modestly, the least amount of avoidable suffering for all; and further, that unavoidable suffering – such as hunger in times of unavoidable shortage of food – should be distributed as equally as possible.)'[5]

[5] *The Open Society and Its Enemies*, vol. i, pp. 284–285.

Such an approach, Popper rightly claims, leads to a perpetual stream of demands for immediate action to remedy
identifiable wrongs. And such action is of a kind most likely
to secure widespread agreement, and result in manifest improvement. He is also, and again rightly, anxious to avoid
Utopianism, which in practice is intolerant and authoritarian (this point will be returned to at greater length in the
next chapter). There is, however, some doubt as to whether
'Minimize unhappiness' goes far enough to be our chief
political maxim, for all its great heuristic value. It confines
itself to rectifying abuses and anomalies within an existing
pattern of distribution of power, possessions and opportunity. Taken literally, it would seem to rule out even such
moderate liberal measures as state subsidy of the arts, and
the municipal provision of such things as sports grounds
and swimming baths. So extremely conservative a position
would be an unnatural consequence of Popper's radical
philosophy, at least in an affluent society – it has, indeed,
proved too conservative for even a professional Conservative politician[6] – and Popper himself would not want to
rest on it. We should make it a methodological rule always
to apply it first, and act on the consequences, but then
wherever possible to look at the situation afresh, in terms
of a second, richer formulation which subsumes our first
one. The second formulation is: 'Maximize the freedom of
individuals to live as they wish'. This requires massive public provision in education, the arts, housing, health, and
every other aspect of social life – but always with the effect
of extending the range of choice, and hence the freedom,
open to individuals.

[6] Sir Edward Boyle: *New Society*, 12.9.1963.

7 The Enemies of the Open Society

Although in my view the most importantly relevant aspect for today of *The Open Society and Its Enemies* is its philosophy of social democracy, and although this was close to Popper's heart when he wrote the book, it was not his chief reason for writing it. One has to remember that for most of the period while he was working on it Hitler was meeting with success after success, conquering almost the whole of Europe, country by country, and driving deep into Russia. Western civilization was confronted with the immediate threat of a new Dark Age. In these circumstances what Popper was concerned to do was to understand and explain the appeal of totalitarian ideas, and do everything he could to undermine it, and also to promulgate the value and importance of liberty in the widest sense. This capacious programme places the philosophy of social democracy in the most unparochial of contexts, unparochial in time as well as in place.

Near the centre of Popper's explanation of the appeal of totalitarianism is a socio-psychological concept which he calls 'the strain of civilization' – a concept related, as he acknowledges, to that formulated by Freud in *Civilization and Its Discontents*. We often hear it asserted that most people do not really want freedom, because freedom involves responsibility, and most people are frightened of responsibility. Whether or not this applies to 'most people' there is, I am sure, a vital element of truth in it. Accepting responsibility for our lives involves continually facing difficult choices and decisions, and bearing the consequences of them when they are wrong, and this is burdensome, not to say alarming. And there is something in all of us, something infantile perhaps, which would like to escape it by having the load taken from our shoulders. However, our strongest instinct being the instinct for survival, our strongest need is probably the need for security; so we are prepared to shift responsibility only to someone or something in whom we have greater confidence than in ourselves. (This is why people want their rulers to be 'better' than themselves, and why they embrace so many implausible beliefs that reinforce confidence that this is so, and why they are so seriously disturbed by revelations that it is not so.) We want the unavoidable and difficult decisions that govern our lives to be taken by someone stronger than ourselves who nevertheless has our interests at heart, as might a stern but benevolent father; or else to be given to us by a practical system of thought that is wiser than we and makes fewer or no mistakes. Above all we want release from fear. And in the end most fears – including the most basic such as fear of the dark, fear of strangers, fear of death, fear of the consequences of our actions and fear of the future – are forms of fear of the unknown. So we are all the time pressing for assurances that the unknown is known really, and that what it contains is something we are going to want anyway. We embrace religions which assure us that we shall not die, and political philosophies which assure us that society will become perfect in the future, perhaps quite soon.

These needs were met by the unchanging certainties of pre-critical societies, with their authority, hierarchy, ritual, tabu and so on. But with the emergence of man from tribalism and the beginnings of the critical tradition, new and frightening demands began to be made : that the individual should question authority, question what he had always taken for granted, and assume responsibility for himself and for others. By contrast with the old certainties, this threatened society with disruption and the individual with disorientation. As a result there was from the beginning a reaction against it, both in society at large and (this was partly Freud's point) within each individual. We purchase freedom at the cost of security, equality at the cost of our self-esteem, and critical self-awareness at the cost of our peace of mind. The price is steep : none of us pays it happily, and many do not want to pay it at all. The best of the Greeks were in no doubt about the merits of the exchange : and better − it has since been said of the greatest of their social critics and questioners − to be Socrates discontented than a pig contented. Yet there was a reaction in which Socrates was put to death for his questioning. And from his pupil Plato onwards there has never been any lack of outstandingly gifted individuals opposed to society's becoming more 'open'. They have wanted it to go back, or forward, to one which was more 'closed'.

So from the beginning of critical thought, with the pre-Socratics, the developing tradition of civilization has had running parallel to it (or perhaps it would be more accurate to say running *within* it) a tradition of reaction against the strain of civilization, which produced accompanying philosophies of return to the womblike security of a precritical or tribal society, or of advance to a Utopia. Because such reactionary and Utopian ideals meet similar needs they have deep and essential affinities. Both reject existing society and proclaim that a more perfect one is to be found at some other point in time. Hence both tend to be violent and yet romantic. If you think society is going from bad to worse you will want to arrest the processes of change; if you regard yourself as establishing the perfect society of the future you will want to perpetuate that society when you get it, and this likewise will mean arresting the processes of change; so both the reactionary and the Utopian are aiming for an arrested society. And since change could only conceivably be prevented by the most rigid social control − by stopping people from doing anything on their own initiative which might have serious social consequences −

both are led into totalitarianism. This development is inherent from the beginning, though when it comes about people will say that the theory has been perverted. It is already commonplace to hear it said of this or that reactionary theory (e.g. that the most efficient form of government would be a dictatorship) or theory of a perfect future (e.g. Communism) that it is all very fine as a theory but unfortunately does not work out in practice. This is a fallacy. If a theory fails to work in practice this alone shows that something is wrong with the theory. (Such, quite apart from anything else, is the point of scientific experiment.)

But although the practical consequences of reactionary and Utopian theories are societies like those of Hitler and Stalin, the desire for a perfect society is clearly not itself rooted in human wickedness, but the reverse. The most horrific excesses have been perpetrated with sincere moral conviction by idealists whose intentions were wholly good; like those, for example, of the Spanish Inquisition. The ideological and religious autocracies and wars that constitute so much of Western history are the most biting exemplification of the proverb 'the road to hell is paved with good intentions'. Nor is it only fools who are led along this path: indeed the sense of dissatisfaction with existing society which starts people off is more likely to go with intelligence and imagination than with their absence – the unintelligent and unimaginative tend rather to accept things as they find them, and to be conservative. So the revolt against civilization – that is to say against the realities of freedom and tolerance, and their consequences in diversity, conflict, the acceptance of unpredictable and uncontrollable change, and manifold insecurity – has, as I suggested earlier, been spearheaded by some of the greatest among the intellectual leaders of mankind. And their genius has made élitism – a contempt for the inert conservatism of ordinary people, and hence a practical non-acceptance of egalitarianism and democracy – all the more 'natural' for them, and them all the more comfortable in it. Popper, in his attacks on the enemies of the open society, attributes to most of them the highest of motives, and to some of them the highest of intelligence, and acknowledges that their appeal is to some of our finest instincts, and to insecurities deep in us all.

He takes Plato as the supreme example of a philosopher of genius whose political theory embodies a wish to return to the past, and incorporates an extensive and detailed critique of it in the first of the two volumes of *The Open Society and Its Enemies*. The second volume contains a corresponding critique of Marx as the supreme philosopher whose theory projects a perfect future. (He distinguishes Marxism from Utopian theories for reasons which will become clear later, but he argues out his opposition to both.) His way of tackling these heavyweight opponents, especially Marx, constitutes in itself one of the most important lessons in method to be gained from his writings. Throughout the history of advocacy and controversy the approach even of polemicists of genius, like Voltaire, has been to seek out and attack the weak points in an opponent's case. This has a severe disadvantage. Every case has weaker as well as stronger parts, and its appeal lies, obviously, in the latter; so to attack the former may embarrass its adherents but not undermine the considerations on which their adherence largely rests. This is one of the reasons why people so rarely change their views after losing an argument. More often such a reverse leads eventually to a strengthening of their position, in that it leads them to abandon or improve the weakest parts of their case. It often happens that the longer two intelligent people go on arguing the better each side's case becomes, for each is being all the time improved by the other's criticism. The Popperian analysis of this is self-evident. What Popper aims to do, and at his best does do, is to seek out and attack an opponent's case at its strongest. Indeed, before attacking it he tries to strengthen it still further. He sees if any of its weaknesses can be removed and any of its formulations improved on, gives it the benefit of every doubt, passes over any obvious loopholes; and then, having got it into the best-argued form he can, attacks it at its most powerful and appealing. This method, the most intellectually serious possible, is thrilling; and its results, when successful, are devastating. For no perceptible version of the defeated case is reconstructable in the light of the criticism, every known resource and reserve of substance being already present in the demolished version. This is what Popper is thought to have done with Marxism – hence the comment from Isaiah Berlin quoted in the second sentence of this book. And I must confess I do not see how any rational man can have read Popper's critique of Marx and still be a Marxist. But that is something we shall come to in a moment.

In the academic world the most controversial aspect of *The Open Society and Its Enemies* has always been the attack on Plato. All too much of the comment on this has been ignorant. I have heard many talk who assumed that the first volume of *The Open Society* primarily is a critique of Plato, that Popper takes a disparaging view of Plato's stature as a philosopher, and that he has been 'totally rebutted', or some such phrase, in Ronald B. Levinson's excellent, massive and scholarly book *In Defense of Plato* (to which Popper made reply in an Addendum to the fourth edition, 1961, of *The Open Society*). None of these things is true. Popper describes Plato unequivocally as 'the greatest philosopher of all time' (p. 98), and uses, naturally and without irony, phrases like 'with all the might of his unequalled intelligence' (p. 109). He does in fact subscribe to Whitehead's dictum that the whole of Western philosophy is footnotes to Plato. Nor is criticism of Plato his primary purpose: Levinson states the position correctly when he writes, on p. 17 of *In Defense of Plato*, 'Popper's attack upon Plato is the negative aspect of his own positive conviction, which motivates his entire book, that the greatest of all revolutions is the transition from the "closed society" to the "open society", an association of free individuals respecting each others' rights within the framework of mutual protection supplied by the state, and achieving, through the making of responsible, rational decisions, a growing measure of humane and enlightened life.' And far from totally rebutting Popper's judgment of Plato, Levinson concludes by conceding the most important part of it. 'First and foremost we have agreed that Plato was proposing, in Popper's terms, to "close" his society, in so far as this denotes regimentation of the ordinary citizens (p. 571). . . . Plato's political ideal can be classified without distortion as a very highly differentiated one among the many varieties of authoritarian governments denoted by our generalized version of Webster's definition of totalitarianism; it can also, as we earlier agreed, be called "totalitarian" in Sabine's carefully guarded sense of a government which "obliterates the distinction between areas of private judgment and of public control".' (p. 573.) Levinson disagrees pungently with a great many things Popper says, yet always with respect for his 'wide and detailed acquaintance with many fields of thought' and 'his unqualified commitment to liberal and democratic ideals, to the defence of which the entire work [*The Open Society and Its Enemies*] is dedicated' (p. 19). The persisting notion that Popper's Platonic scholarship has somehow been shown to be rubbishy is itself rubbishy in the sense that it is reiterated without knowledge. The more important philosophers are not guilty, however. Bertrand Russell wrote: 'His attack on Plato, while unorthodox, is in my opinion thoroughly justified'. And Gilbert Ryle, himself a notable Plato scholar, wrote in his review of Popper's book in *Mind*: 'His studies in Greek history and Greek thought have obviously been profound and original. Platonic exegesis will never be the same again'. A quarter of a century later, on BBC Radio 3 (28 July 1972) Ryle specifically re-endorsed this judgment.

Platonism as such is not a live issue in the political and social life of the modern world. Nor is the philosophy of the pre-Socratics. But Marxism is. In fact in one overwhelmingly practical respect the personal achievement of Marx as represented by the situation of our time is without parallel in the history of mankind. Less than a hundred years ago, there he was, an intellectual in his fifties, living in Hampstead with his wife and family, devoting his days to reading and writing, little known to even the educated public. And in under seventy years of his death a third of the entire human race, including the whole of Russia and its empire, and the whole of China, had adopted forms of society which called themselves by his name. It is a phenomenon whose utter extraordinariness is still, I think, insufficiently pondered. But few would deny that Marx is the most influential philosopher of the last hundred years, and that an understanding of the world we live in today is impossible without some knowledge of his political and social thought. And, unlike twenty years ago, today interest in Marxism is increasing, not diminishing, in our universities and among the intelligent young throughout the West.

Central to Marxism is its claim to be scientific. Marx saw himself as, so to speak, the Newton or Darwin of the historical, political, economic -- in fact what one might generally call the social -- sciences. He offered to dedicate the second volume of *Das Kapital* to Darwin, 'for whom he had a greater intellectual admiration than for any other of his contemporaries, regarding him as having, by his theory of evolution and natural selection, done for the morphology of the natural sciences, what he himself was striving to do for human history. Darwin hastily declined the honour in a polite, cautiously phrased letter, saying that he was unhappily ignorant of economic science, but offered the author his good wishes in what he assumed to be their common end – the advancement of human knowledge.'[1] The heart of the matter is this: Marx believed that the development of human societies was governed by scientific laws of which he was the discoverer. His conception of science was unavoidably pre-Einsteinian. Like every other well-informed man of his time he thought that Newton had discovered Natural Laws which govern the motions of matter in space, so that given the relevant data about any physical system one could predict all its future states. Thus we can predict the times of sunrise and sunset, eclipses, the movements of tides, and so on. However, although Natural Laws enable us to foretell the future of our solar system they do not enable us to control it: they work, it might be said, with iron necessity towards inevitable results which we can scientifically predict and describe but not alter. Marx saw his own discoveries as paralleling this precisely, and he drew the parallel by a deliberate use of Newtonian terms. In *Das Kapital* he describes himself as having discovered 'the Natural Laws of capitalist production', and warns that 'even when a society has got upon the right track for the discovery of the Natural Laws of its movement – and it is the ultimate aim of this work to lay bare the Economic Law of Motion of modern society – it can neither clear by bold leaps, nor remove by legal enactments, the obstacles offered by the successive phases of its normal development.... It is a question of these laws themselves, of these tendencies working with iron necessity towards inevitable results. The country that is more developed industrially only shows, to the less developed, the image of its own future.'

The fact that Marx personally welcomed the future which he saw as inevitable is scientifically irrelevant. Strictly speaking he could no more be said to be advocating it than an astronomer is advocating the eclipses he predicts, though he may enjoy watching them when they happen,

[1] Isaiah Berlin, *Karl Marx*, p. 232.

and so look forward to them and be pleased at their coming. At all times Marx was insistent that his theory was 'scientific' in this sense – he was describing, not prescribing: and he dismissed other forms of Socialism by contrast as 'Utopian' – at best mere advocacy, at worst mere visions. Popper accepts this distinction between, on the one hand, the Marxist belief that we are powerless to shape the course of history, and on the other hand Utopian beliefs that it is in our power to make a perfect society – though Marxism has been widely misunderstood as being a belief of the latter kind, and seems actually to be thought so by most Communists, who are thus what Popper would term 'vulgar Marxists' and what Marx would have termed 'Utopian Socialists'. The truth is, I think, that Communism is Utopian and Marxism not, which makes it important to keep the distinction in mind.

A crucial consequence of Marxism's claim to be science is that it must defend itself successfully at a scientific level of argument or else lapse into incoherence. And if it suffers defeat at any point on this level, it has no recourse to other forms of argument: it must, in short, submit itself to tests and accept the consequences. And what Popper is thought to have done is demolish its claims to scientific truth beyond any serious possibility of their reconstitution. He has not done this by showing Marx's theory to be unfalsifiable. Vulgar Marxism is unfalsifiable, but Popper does not make the mistake of attributing vulgar Marxism to Marx. Karl Marx's own theory, treated with the intellectual seriousness it deserves, yielded a considerable number of falsifiable predictions, the most important of which have now been falsified. For instance, according to the theory only fully developed Capitalist countries could go Communist, and therefore all societies would have to complete the Capitalist stage of development first: but in fact, except for Czechoslovakia, all the countries to have gone Communist have been pre-industrial – none has been a fully developed Capitalist society. According to the theory the revolution would have to be based on the industrial proletariat : but Mao Tse-Tung, Ho Chi-Minh and Fidel Castro explicitly rejected this and based successful revolutions on the peasantries of their different countries. According to the theory there are elaborate reasons why the industrial proletariat must inevitably get poorer, more numerous, more class-conscious and more revolutionary : in fact, in all industrial countries since Marx's day, it has become richer, less numerous, less class-conscious and less revolutionary. According to the theory Communism could be brought about only by the workers themselves, the masses : in fact in no country to this day, not even Chile, has the Communist party managed to get the support of the majority in a free election; where they have achieved full power it has been imposed on the majority by an army, usually a foreign one. According to the theory, ownership of the Capitalist means of production was bound to become concentrated in fewer and fewer hands : in fact, with the development of the joint-stock company, ownership has become so widely dispersed that control has passed into the hands of a new class of professional managers. And the emergence of this class is itself a refutation of the Marxist prediction that all other classes would inevitably disappear and be polarized into two, an ever shrinking Capitalist class which owned and controlled but did not work, and an ever expanding proletariat which worked but did not own or control.

And then, to take up a different tack, what Marx and Engels had to say about most sciences has been rendered obsolete by the subsequent development of those sciences : for instance their theory of matter by post-Einsteinian physics, and their understanding of individual behaviour by post-Freudian psychology. The Ricardian economic foundations of Marxism itself have been swept into limbo by post-Keynesian economics, and its Hegelian logical foundations by post-Frege logic. Their view of the future development of political institutions was quite unlike what has actually occurred – chiefly, I suspect, because of their failure to take the growth of parliamentary democracy seriously (a failure again imposed on them by their theory, which precluded any such serious development).

All this constitutes the refutation of a theory claiming to be scientific by the basic method of submitting its predictions to the test of experience and finding them falsified. But it will be remembered from earlier chapters that this, though the main, is not the only kind of test a theory has to pass: it has also to meet the logical criteria of internal consistency and coherence. And Marxism's fundamental tenet that the development of the means of production is the sole determinant of historical change is shown to be logically incoherent by the fact that no such theory can explain how it is that the means of production do develop instead of remaining the same.

Marx's view that history develops according to scientific laws is one example of what Popper calls 'historicism'. 'I mean by "historicism" an approach to the social sciences which assumes that *historical prediction* is their principal aim, and which assumes that this aim is attainable by discovering the "rhythms" or the "patterns", the "laws" or the "trends" that underlie the evolution of history.'[2] Examples of historicist beliefs are: that of the Old Testament Jews in the mission of the Chosen People; that of the early Christians in the inevitability of mass conversions to be followed by the Second Coming; that of some Romans in the destiny of Rome to rule the world; that of Enlightenment liberals in the inevitability of progress and the perfectibility of man; that of so many Socialists in the inevitability of Socialism; that of Hitler in the establishment of a Thousand Year Reich. One has only to start listing some of the more famous examples to note their low fruition-rate. But apart from specific theories, the general notion that history must

[2] *The Poverty of Historicism*, p. 3.

have a destination, or if not that a plot, or at any rate a meaning, or at least some sort of coherent pattern, seems to be widespread.

If historical inevitability is to be seriously argued a limited number of explanations is possible. Either history is being directed by some outside intelligence (usually God) in accordance with its own purposes. Or history is being driven forward by some *inside* intelligence (immanent spirit, life force or some such entity as 'the destiny of man'). Or there is no spirit at all, in which case entirely deterministic material processes must be at work. The first two alternatives are in an obvious sense metaphysical : they are not falsifiable, and certainly not scientific. And the third rests on a conception of science which is no longer tenable.

The reasons for Popper's rejection of these views should be clear from everything that has gone before in this book. He is an indeterminist who believes that change is the result of our attempts to solve our problems – and that our attempts to solve our problems involve, among other unpredictables, imagination, choice and luck. Of these we are responsible for our choices. Insofar as any process of direction is at work it is we, in our interaction with each other, and with our physical environment (which we as a species have not created) and with World 3 (which we as a species have created, but which each individual inherits and can do only a little to change) who move history forward. Any purposes it embodies are our purposes. Any meaning it has is meaning we give it.

From the standpoint of these ideas he attacks all historicist theories. And the one on which he mounts his most powerful attack is Marxism, both because it is the most influential of them in the modern world and because it is the one above all which claims that the development of history takes place according to scientific laws, and that knowledge of these laws (which it provides) enables us to predict the future. Popper's argument at its most technical consists in showing that no scientific predictor, whether a human scientist or a calculating machine, can possibly predict, by scientific methods, its own future results. In more homely terms the argument takes the following tack. It is easy to show that the course of human history has been strongly influenced by the growth of human knowledge, a fact which even people who regard all knowledge as the by-product of material development can admit without self-contradiction. But it is logically impossible to predict future knowledge: if we could predict future knowledge we would have it now, and it would not be future; if we could predict future discoveries they would be present discoveries. From this it follows that if the future contains any significant discoveries at all it is impossible to predict it scientifically, even if it is determined independently of human wishes. And there is another argument: if the future were scientifically predictable it could not, once discovered, remain secret, since it would in principle be rediscoverable by anybody. This would furthermore present us with a paradox about the possibility/impossibility of taking evasive action. On these logical grounds alone historicism collapses; and we must reject the notion, central to the Marxist programme, of a theoretical history corresponding to theoretical physics.

With the collapse of the notion that the future is scientifically predictable the notion of the totally planned society goes down as well. This is also shown to be logically incoherent in other ways: first, because it cannot give a consistent answer to the question 'Who plans the planners?'; and second because, as has been shown, our actions in any case are likely to have unintended consequences. This latter point, incidentally, exposes the fallacy in the assumption made by Utopians generally (though not by Marx – indeed Marxism is clearer about this than many Social Democrats) that 'when something "bad" happens in society, something we dislike, such as war, poverty, unemployment, then it must be the result of some bad intention, some sinister design : somebody has done it "on purpose"; and, of course, somebody profits from it. I have called this philosophical assumption the conspiracy theory of society.[3] Other fronts in Popper's onslaught on Marxism are supported by arguments which have been expounded earlier in this book and need not be repeated, the most important being that Marx, in putting forward what he called 'scientific Socialism', was wrong not only about society but also about science, his view of it being the one Popper believes himself to have overthrown. If Popper is right about science then his is also the only genuinely scientific political philosophy; and also, most importantly, the hostility to science and the revolt against reason, both of which are so prominently expressed in today's world, are directed at false conceptions of science and reason.

Popper's arguments that we can know of no meaning in history other than that invested in it by human beings have a psychologically disturbing, because disorienting, effect on some people who feel themselves placed in some sort of existentialist void by them. Others fear that if Popper is right all values and norms must be arbitrary. The latter misapprehension is well dealt with in *The Open Society* (vol. i, pp. 64–65). 'Nearly all misunderstandings can be traced back to one fundamental misapprehension, namely, to the belief that "convention" implies "arbitrariness"; that if we are free to choose any system of norms we like, then one system is just as good as any other. It must, of course, be admitted that the view that norms are conventional or artificial indicates that there will be a certain element of arbitrariness involved, i.e. that there may be different systems of norms between which there is not much to choose (a fact that has been duly emphasized by Protagoras). But artificiality by no means implies full arbitrariness. Mathematical calculi, for instance, or symphonies, or plays,

[3] Popper in *Modern British Philosophy* (ed. Bryan Magee), p. 67.

are highly artificial, yet it does not follow that one calculus or symphony or play is just as good as any other.' His full explanation of why not, and of what he believes to be man's true orientation, is provided by his evolutionary theory of knowledge, in particular his theory of World 3, which is to be found in writings discussed by us earlier, though published by him later.

Some of Popper's arguments against Marxism apply to Utopianism – for instance his argument against the possibility of societies being 'swept away' and replaced by something 'wholly new'. 'The Utopian approach may be described as follows. Any rational action must have a certain aim. It is rational in the same degree as it pursues its aim consciously and consistently, and as it determines its means according to this end. To choose the end is therefore the first thing we have to do if we wish to act rationally; and we must be careful to determine our real or ultimate ends, from which we must distinguish clearly those intermediate or partial ends which actually are only means, or steps on the way, to the ultimate end. If we neglect this distinction, then we must also neglect to ask whether these partial ends are likely to promote the ultimate end, and accordingly, we must fail to act rationally. These principles, if applied to the realm of political activity, demand that we must determine our ultimate political aim, or the Ideal State, before taking any practical action. Only when this ultimate aim is determined, in rough outline at least, only when we are in possession of something like a blueprint of the society at which we aim, only then can we begin to consider the best ways and means for its realization, and to draw up a plan for practical action.'[4]

Popper's arguments against any approach to politics which starts from a blueprint and then sets out to actualize it have to be faced by any idealist if he seriously wants to be an idealist without illusions. There is first the argument

[4] *The Open Society and Its Enemies*, vol. i, p. 157.

that wherever you want to go you have no choice but to start from where you are. It is no more possible to start from scratch in politics than it is in epistemology or science or the arts. All real, as distinct from envisaged, change can only be change in actually existing circumstances. Utopians commonly assert that before this or that thing can be changed, society as a whole will have to be changed; but what this comes down to is the assertion that before you can change anything you must change everything, which is self-contradictory. Second, whatever actions we take will have some unintended consequences which may easily be at odds with our blueprint. And the more wholesale the action the more plentiful the unintended consequences. To claim rationality for sweeping plans to change society as a whole is to claim a degree of detailed sociological knowledge which we simply do not possess. And to talk in the Utopian way about means and ends is to use a metaphor misleadingly: what is actually in question is one set of events close in time, which are referred to as 'the means', followed by another more distant set of events, which are called 'the end'. But these will be followed in turn – unless history just stops – by yet further successive sets of events. So the end is not an end in fact, and there can be no serious defence for privileges claimed for what is merely the second set of events in an endless series. What is more the first set of events, being closer in time, are more likely to materialize in the form envisaged than the second, more distant and more uncertain. Rewards promised by the latter are less sure than the sacrifices made for them in the former. And if all individuals have equal moral claims it is wrong to sacrifice one generation to the next.

As to the blueprint itself, it is an ascertainable fact that people differ about the kind of society they want – even conventional Conservatives, Liberals and Socialists do so, to allow for no others. So whatever the nature of the group that gets into power with the aim of putting its blueprint into production it will have to render the opposition of others ineffective, if not coerce them into serving an end they disagree with. Whereas a free society cannot impose common social purposes, a government with utopian aims has to, and is bound to become authoritarian. The radical reconstruction of society is a huge undertaking which is bound to take a long time: is it even remotely likely that social objectives and ideas and ideals will not substantially change during that time, especially as it will be, by definition, a time of revolutionary upheaval? Yet if they do change it means that what appeared the most desirable form of society, even to the people who made the blueprint, will diverge further and further from it as they approach it – and further still from anything wanted by their successors, who had nothing to do with making the blueprint in the first place. This is related to another argument, to the effect that not only are the planners themselves part of the society they wish to sweep away but their social experience, and therefore social assumptions and aims, however critical, are bound to have been deeply conditioned by it. So *really* sweeping it away includes sweeping them and their plans away too. In any case a social reconstruction which is radical and, because radical, prolonged, is bound to uproot and disorient very large numbers of people, thereby creating widespread psychological as well as material adversity; and one must expect at least some people to oppose measures that threaten them with these effects. Such people will be seen by the power-holders trying to actualize the ideal society as opposing the wholly good out of self-interest – and there will be half a truth in this. So they will be seen as enemies of society. Inevitably this will make them victims in what follows. For ideal goals, being unattainable, are a long time coming, and the period over which criticism and opposition have to be stifled is prolonged more and more; so intolerance and authoritarianism will intensify, albeit with the best of intentions. And precisely because intentions and goals are thought to be ideal the persistent failure of the latter to materialize is bound to give rise to accusations that someone is rocking the boat – there must be sabotage, or foreign interference, or corrupt leadership, for all possible explanations that rule out criticism of the revolution involve malignity on somebody's part. So it becomes necessary to identify culprits, and to root them out; and if culprits there must be, culprits will be found. By now the revolutionary regime will be up to its neck in the unforeseen consequences of its actions. For even after enemies of the revolution have received their deserts the revolutionary goals will obstinately go on not materializing; and the ruling group will be driven more and more to grasping at immediate solutions to urgent problems (what Popper calls 'unplanned planning') which is usually one of the things for which they most despised their predecessor regimes. This will open yet wider the disparity between their declared aims and what they are actually doing – the latter more and more coming to resemble the activities of the most cynically unutopian governments.

The fact is, of course, that nearly all of us require the most important aspects of the social order to continue functioning through any reconstruction: people must continue to be fed and clothed and housed and kept warm; children, if they are not to be intolerably victimized, must continue to be cared for and educated; transport, medical, police and fire services must continue to operate. And in a modern society these things depend on large-scale organization. To sweep it all away at once would be to create, literally, a chaos; and to believe that somehow out of *that* an ideal society would emerge borders on the mad, as does even the belief that a society merely better than the one we have now is more likely to emerge from chaos than from the society we have now. However, even if we were determined to, we could never, despite our dreams of perfection, sweep everything away and begin again. Mankind is like the crew of a ship at sea who can choose to remodel any part of the ship they live in, and can remodel it entirely section by section, but cannot remodel it all at once.

The fact that change is never going to stop renders the very notion of a blueprint for the good society nonsensical, for even if society became like the blueprint it would instantly begin to depart from it. So not only are ideal societies unattainable because they are ideal, they are unattainable also because, to correspond to any sort of blueprint at all, they would have to be static, fixed, unchanging; and no foreseeable society is going to be those things. Indeed, the pace of social change seems to get faster, not slower, with every year that passes. And the process is going to have, so far as we can see, no end. So to have any hope at all of corresponding to the realities a political approach must be concerned not with states of affairs but with change. Our task is not the impossible one of establishing and preserving a particular form of society: it is to maximize our control over the actual changes that occur in a process of change which is never-ending – and to use that control wisely.

And because society will never be perfect, to raise questions like 'What is the ideal form of society?' is academic. Indeed, Popper condemns 'what is?' questions generally: 'What is gravity?' and 'What is life?' are as irrelevant to making progress in science (see pp. 34 and 49) as 'what is freedom?' and 'What is justice?' are to making progress in politics. Equally to be condemned are 'What is?' questions disguised by being at one remove – for instance 'Is Britain really a democracy?' which leads straight to 'What do you mean by democracy?' or 'What is democracy?'. Their quasi-magical attempt to capture the essence of reality in a definition has led Popper to brand the use of such questions as 'essentialism'. In politics the essentialist approach leads almost naturally to Utopianism and doctrinal conflict. Genuinely important questions are more like 'What should we do in these circumstances? What are your proposals?' To them the answers can be fruitfully discussed and criticized; and then, if they stand up to that, tried out. Nothing that is not a proposal can ever be put into practice. So what matters in politics, as in science, is not the analysis of concepts but the critical discussion of theories, and their subjection to the tests of experience.

Because authoritarian structures incorporate the same mistaken notions of certainty, and the same mistaken assumptions about method, as does the traditional view of science, the arguments underlying Popper's criticism of the view that in politics we even can, let alone should aim to, establish and preserve a certain state of society are in point after point the same as those underlying his criticism of the view that science even can, let alone should aim to, establish and preserve certain knowledge. And his view, by contrast, that science *is* scientific method, and his view of how that method is to be seen, are at all levels interrelated with his view that politics is political method, and his view of how *that* method is to be seen. In both cases what he asks us to use with imagination and feeling is an unending feedback process in which the bold propounding of new ideas is invariably attended by their subjection to rigorous error elimination in the light of experience. He calls this approach 'critical rationalism' in philosophy; in politics he calls it, 'piecemeal social engineering'. This phrase is trebly unfortunate: 'piecemeal' is usually pejorative anyway, and here it has the additional disadvantage of masking the radicalism of the method proposed; and 'engineering' has unpleasant connotations when applied to human beings. It sounds heartless, but nothing could be more passionate than Popper's advocacy of it, or more humane than some of his arguments. In trying to show how his philosophy is all of a piece I have concentrated in this book on the logical arguments and their interrelationships, but even more important are the moral arguments; and for these, as for so much else that we have not dealt with, the reader is advised to turn to Popper's books.

Postscript

Since this book was written, a massive two-volume appraisal of Popper's life work has appeared in the Library of Living Philosophers, edited by P. A. Schilpp and published in 1974 by the Open Court Press, La Salle, Illinois. It is in four parts: the first, almost a book in itself, is an intellectual autobiography by Popper; the second consists of 33 critical articles on his work by various distinguished figures; the third is his 'Reply to My Critics'; and the fourth is the most complete bibliography of his work so far published.

Something should be said in conclusion about Popper's unpublished work. The first book he wrote, *Die beiden Grundprobleme der Erkenntnistheorie (The Two Fundamental Problems of Epistemology)*, is only now being prepared for the press in Germany. No doubt an English translation will appear one day. When his second book to be written and first to be published, *Logik der Forschung*, was due to appear in English 25 years after its appearance in German, Popper wanted to add a postscript about the respects in which his views had in the meantime changed. This grew under his pen to such an extent that it became a substantial book in its own right: so *The Logic of Scientific Discovery* appeared without it, and *Postscript* has remained in galley proof since 1957. In my judgment it is as important as his other books – in particular, its Metaphysical Epilogue is among the finest things he has written – and the sooner it appears the better.

But the fact is that Popper has published, as yet, little more than half his work. There are extensive – that is to say book-length, or near book-length – unpublished writings on Einstein's theory of relativity, Popper's theory of World 3 and the body-mind problem, evolution, and his philosophy of language; and a wealth of single articles and lectures on other questions. And apart from this, he is still doing new work. So although he is now in his seventies the amount of work yet to be set before the public is so great that his philosophy must be thought of as a still developing one.

Bibliography

Books by Karl Popper

The Logic of Scientific Discovery, Hutchinson, first published 1959, latest revised (third) edition 1972. This is an English translation, with new footnotes and appendices, of *Logik der Forschung*, first published in Vienna in 1934 (dated 1935), fifth edition Tübingen 1973.

The Open Society and Its Enemies, Routledge & Kegan Paul, two volumes, first published 1945, latest revised (fifth) edition 1966.

The Poverty of Historicism, Routledge & Kegan Paul, first published in book form 1957, corrected edition 1961.

Conjectures and Refutations: the Growth of Scientific Knowledge, Routledge & Kegan Paul, first published 1963, latest revised (fourth) edition 1972.

Objective Knowledge: an Evolutionary Approach, Oxford University Press, first published 1972, reprinted with corrections 1973, latest corrected edition 1975.

See also his contributions to *Modern British Philosophy* by Bryan Magee, Secker & Warburg, first published 1971; and to *The Philosophy of Karl Popper*, Open Court Press, La Salle, Illinois, first published 1974.

N.B. All the above books except the last are available in soft as well as hard covers.

Wittgenstein
David Pears

The work of Ludwig Wittgenstein is a strange product of hard reasoning and brilliant imagination, immediately captivating but deep and often difficult to fathom. Besides, Wittgenstein produced not one but two highly original philosophies at different times in his life. Both must be understood, and reconciled; and it is a reconciliation as well as an exposition that David Pears offers in this book. He analyses Wittgenstein's two major works—the *Tractatus Logico-Philosophicus* and the *Philosophical Investigations*—emphasises their limitations as well as their merits, and sets his conclusion against the background of the striking changes in the nature of philosophy in this century.

'This is one of the best studies of Wittgenstein that has yet appeared . . . subtle and intricate work, wide in scope and rigorously argued.'
The Spectator

'. . . finely, and often most felicitously, written . . . Pears succeeds in conveying the point of these issues of logic with an amazing expository tact that totally avoids an infestation of the pages with formal symbolism.'
The Sunday Times

Memories, Dreams, Reflections

C. G. Jung

Until near the end of his long life, Jung steadfastly refused to attempt the autobiography which his friends and disciples urged him to write and his admirers throughout the world hoped for from him. What he had to say, he maintained, was to be found in the twenty volumes of his professional writings. However, in 1957 he agreed to provide his friend and assistant of many years standing, Aniela Jaffe, with the necessary material and exercise a responsible supervision over what she wrote. Soon the task so fascinated him that he began doing the writing himself; and the manuscript as he left it on his death in 1961 is very largely from his own hand. The result is a unique memoir of the inner life of a great and original genius.

'Jung's single-minded humility, his passion to unearth truth, is one of the loveliest impressions to emerge from this absorbing and many-sided book.' *The Times*

'He was on a giant scale . . . he was a master of the soul in his insights, a profound sage in his conclusions. He is also one of Western Man's great liberators.' J. B. Priestley, *Sunday Telegraph*

'Can sometimes rise to the heights of a Blake or a Nietzsche or a Kierkegaard . . . like any true prophet or artist extended the range of the human imagination . . . to be able to share Jungian emotions is surely an almost necessary capacity of the free mind.' Philip Toynbee, *Observer*